SIGHT TO SOUND

by Leon White

Acknowledgements

For help in preparing this book I must thank Mike Warren, Tom Runyan, Ted Greene, Dale Zdenek, and Jay Graydon. Editing and proof reading by Judy White and Jennie Gillespie. All proof copies by Len Mosk and Copymat, North Hollywood, California. Special thanks to Tony Mandracchia. Photography by Studio Nine, Costa Mesa, California. Title and cover concept by Jon Devirian. Studio: courtesy Village Recorders, Westwood, CA.

DALE ZDENEK PUBLICATIONS

D1211046

EL 2786

Dedicated to Judy and Walter White

TABLE OF CONTENTS

TO THE TEACHER

This is a method for sight reading music on the guitar. The two main components of playing which we will be dealing with are sound and time. In the section on sound we will locate pitches on paper and on the guitar. Basic definitions, derivations of scales, and position playing will all be covered here. The section on time will include definitions of beat, pulse, and rhythm. Note values will be carefully derived, and time signatures will be explained without the vague "common time" concept.

All basic concepts will be taught through SINGLE LINE PLAYING. Other methods demand that the student become fluent at chord reading before being exposed to difficult rhythmic figures. The ominous appearance of block chords often discourages the student from progressing rhythmically. He fumbles with the chords and confuses the rhythm. Soon the simplest solo line has become an incredible challenge. It is for this reason that we have placed block chord reading at the end of this learning program.

This book is sequentially programmed. New notes or rhythms are introduced individually and drilled on. Each exercise is the logical antecedent of the previous one. The student may progress at his own speed. Every effort has been made to anticipate the questions that a beginning music student might have. We have tried to make the book complete enough to be used as a self instruction method. The exercises have been designed to challenge a student who is adept at 'playing by ear.' There are special sections on tuning and music symbols.

TO THE STUDENT

WHERE WE ARE COMING FROM . . .

Although the guitar is one of today's most popular instruments, formal development of a consistent teaching method, which includes reading, has lagged way behind other instruments of the band and orchestra.

One reason is the origin of the guitar. As a popular "folk" instrument, it received little attention from "classically" trained musicians until recently. In addition the guitar has gone through so many changes both in the technology of its sound and in new styles of music, that the methods for learning have barely begun to catch up with the music being innovated today.

Now, because of its overwhelming popularity and today's music, the guitar has been forced to catch up with the rest of the instruments. There were always people who by unique talent and hard work were able to create, read, and teach very advanced music on the guitar. But the number was very small. The popular demand of today's guitarist, both amateur, and professional, is such that you just can't play three chords and please anybody anymore, not even yourself! In the old days (20 years ago?) reading music was learned on the guitar by sheer repitition, if help was available. Harmony, theory and technique were picked up wherever they could be found. There was no order, logic, or method; it was all experience. In any event the guitar was usually shoved into the rhythm section to help keep time — not a demanding job compared to today's work.

The demand for good reading guitarists has increased because of the integration of the jazz, pop, classical, rock, and country styles of music. You need only go to any recording studio to see how important the ability to read music is. One session may have a classical player, a country picker, and a hard rocker on the same date with strings, brass and a rhythm section. The producer could hardly shout "Blues in F."

If you are creating original music, notating it correctly is important if you wish to communicate it to other musicians. If you can read, no style or type of music can remain a mystery to you. The more you read and explore, the better your playing will become.

WHAT WE HOPE TO DO

The object of this book is to teach students of the guitar how to read music. We want you to be able to read new material with such ease that you can concentrate on giving meaning to the written page, rather than just playing 'the right notes.' We have included concepts of basic harmony with the reading because it is easier to understand and REMEMBER them both when they are learned together. The more you remember, the quicker you'll be able to apply it. In the studio time is money, more than anything else. Playing in the studio requires mental agility in the art of understanding, as well as guitar technique. You must be able to understand someone else's music (or communicate your own) quickly and precisely whether it's on paper, in words, or by playing with the other musicians.

And if you're required to make up a solo on the spot, you better hope you know where the chords and melody are going, or you'll never cut it.

HOW WE HOPE TO DO IT

Reading is simply a mechanical process like walking. It is the coordination of a little knowledge, your hands, and your eye. That's all!! So to help you learn to read, we are going to supply the knowledge, explain the short cuts, and help you get started. The rest is up to you.

To read quickly you must have a firm understanding of harmony and rhythm.

Fifty percent of this book is information organized for easy memory so that you may learn it and IMMEDIATELY apply it. This includes music theory, harmony, rhythm, keys and scales, and how they all fit together.

The following five areas are where our goals lie —

1. You will realize the importance of reading music to see what others have to say.
2. You will learn the vocabulary of music.
3. You will learn the correct notation of music on paper.
4. You will hope you gain enough control over your muscles (technique) to be able to play whatever you might find on the paper.
5. You will be able to find your way around the guitar without looking at it — or, while looking at something else (like the music?)

This method has its roots in a common sense view of your hand, head, and guitar. We have tried to be LOGICAL, and ORDERLY. There are no gimmicks, and there is no magic. You must invest time and energy if you wish to be successful. Many people who have a guitar, play AT it. There is nothing wrong with this. But if you have the desire to experience new music and improve your playing, then you must spend some time STUDYING WITH the guitar. This means working at your own speed, in areas that excite you most, and ENJOYING the whole process. If you feel inadequate in your playing, or unhappy with the guitar, it will always show up in your playing.

For many this book may be the first experience in working with regularity at their playing. It is our hope that you will keep an open mind, be encouraged to experiment, and above all enjoy your effort with music. Please remember that we have included a lot of very basic information. We've done this to try and fill in all the various gaps student guitarists could have. Read everything, and mark any information that's new to you.

CHAPTER 1

FUNDAMENTALS
HOW TO APPROACH YOUR GUITAR

(always from behind so you've got the jump on it if it tries to get away)

This section should get you sat down, strapped, adjusted, tuned, and thinking about your practice time. (Nothing to play yet.)

As you hold the guitar, the 'first string' is closest to the floor. All the strings are numbered, one through six, with the sixth string closest to the ceiling. This numbering is universally accepted in all guitar diagrams and some tableture systems.

Below is a diagram of the guitar fretboard. This diagram is common to guitar methods, and will be useful in locating notes at first.

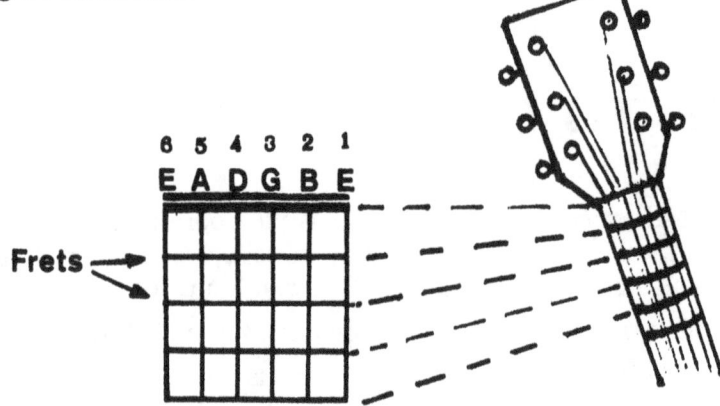

After you have looked at this diagram, learn which strings are which!! The B string is the second, the G is the third, the D is the fourth, the A is the fifth, and the low E is the sixth. The first string is the high E.

TUNING THE GUITAR

(for reference only)

Remember — tuning is one of the hardest things to do. Varying weather conditions, the condition of the guitar, the original quality and the age and condition of the strings, will all fight you to keep the guitar out of tune.

Poor tuning spoils everything you play, so work at it all the time.

Open: Used to describe a string that is not being touched by the left hand, when plucked by the right hand.

Fretted: When the left hand is pushing the string against the neck.

The numbers used with the diagram are there only to help clarify this diagram when learning to "tune up" your guitar. They are NOT standard notation, and the notes are not normally called by this number name.

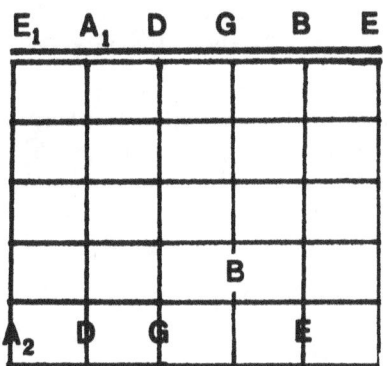

Get E_1 from pitch pipe.

adjust open "A" (A_1) to sound like fretted "A" (A_2).

Adjust open D to sound like fretted D.

Adjust open G to sound like fretted G.

Adjust open B to sound like fretted B.

Adjust open E to sound like fretted B.

The letters are the names of the notes; do not worry about the names now – just learn the procedure.

WARM-UP

Riding in the car, getting out in the rain on a scorching hot day, carrying your guitar, six amplifiers, two fuzz tones and a P.A. system, does not prepare your muscles for delicate and precise movement on the guitar. SO . . .

You should develop a 'warm-up' pattern of scales, chords, riffs, or something that you can do to relax your muscles and 'fine tune' them to play smoothly. Regardless of what you do, it should be simple, slow, smooth, and should move over most of the fingerboard by the time you are done. (Remember the frets are not the same distance apart at the top of the guitar as they are at the other end.)

THE GOAL

The warm-up should be for BOTH hands, and if you can also relax, and begin to focus your MIND on your music you will have a better chance of playing well and satisfying yourself.

THE STRAP

The purpose of the strap is to support your guitar comfortably, whether you are standing or sitting. Much of your 'on the job' READING will be done sitting down, so it is important to find a good sitting posture that will not tire you out.

Sit holding the guitar comfortably in your hands as if playing. Adjust the strap so that the guitar remains in that position when you LET GO of the instrument. The strap should hold the guitar in a way that makes you feel the guitar is just sitting loosely on your lap. Many professionals prefer sitting cross-legged for comfort. (Right leg over left for a right hand player; it takes getting used to.) The strap is doing its job when both arms and wrists are COMPLETELY free to play. When you stand, the guitar should be in the same place, relative to your body. It should require no adjustment. (Do not use straps that contain elastic in them. As the elastic gets old and stretches, the strap will need constant adjustment.) Unless you feel it is absolutely necessary to wear a poisonous snake around your head when performing, do not indulge in extremes in positioning your guitar – that is, no matter who you are, learning to play a guitar hanging around your KNEES is not right. As soon as you sit down, the guitar is in a different position, and all your hand and arm movement must be changed to suit the new location.

THE GOAL

Position the guitar so that you may move freely in your playing motions, whether sitting or standing, without changing the strap.

ABOUT PRACTICING . . .

If you have not done so up till now, you should try and organize your practice time. You have essentially four areas of concentration — LEFT HAND, RIGHT HAND, BRAIN, and EAR AND EYE.

As you begin now, you may not have something to practice in each of these categories. But as you continue your playing you will find exercises and techniques that you will want to practice, and add to your organization. So keep these categories in mind as you continue your playing.

LEFT HAND

Technique in motion is the emphasis here. You should be trying to develop agility and strength in all of the fingers.

RIGHT HAND

Motion across the strings is the main point here. Do you play with your fingers or do you use a pick? How are you holding the pick? Loose wrist or tight? Loose arm or tight? Can you pick both up and down strokes with equal volume and strength? A good teacher may be able to give you some advice here, but the decision rests with you and what works best for you.

BRAIN

This area includes all your knowledge, both musical and non-musical that you apply to your playing. It includes scales, chords, keys, notes, rhythm and dynamics (loud or soft playing), as well as your taste, and attitude towards your music.

EAR AND EYE

Ear and eye is a giant category that is based on recognizing music on paper or in the air, and knowing what is is from either exposure. Being able to quickly recognize notes on paper and knowing a chord progression when you hear it, are just two of the areas that belong in this category.

Needless to say, when you are actually playing, these four major areas are completely interwoven. However, if you are to improve, you must be able to isolate one particular category to focus your work on.

Music reading falls in the categories of "Brain" and "Ear and Eye." It deserves as much attention as you can give it. But . . . do not exclude other areas either. An approximate division of your time might be 25% in each area. Or perhaps you might alternate areas in practice sessions, playing one day more on chords than the day before and so on. You should try different schedules to see what fits you best. However, reading should be done every day, even if only for fifteen minutes. That helps your memory. Remember too, that there will be times when you are all 'wrists' . . . just relax and take a break. The more anger or frustration you involve in your practicing, the less you learn. Good Luck!

ORGANIZING YOUR PRACTICE TIME

Some general rules:

1. Tune your guitar ! ! ! ! ! ! ! ! ! !
2. Warm up slowly and carefully. Try to relax and concentrate on your hands and on a smooth flowing motion. You could spend from two minutes to ten minutes in easy, slow playing for your warm-up.
3. If you do not have time before you perform, or before your lesson, begin whatever you play, with as much care and ease as possible. NEVER sit down, and begin a hard, loud, or fast exercise ! ! ! ! ! ! ! ! ! ! You should have some kind of a rough schedule of how you want to spend your time. FOLLOW IT ! ! ! ! ! If it doesn't work at first, give it a couple of tries. If you still feel uncomfortable, CHANGE IT. It's your time, and your effort, and you should do what you think best to achieve the results you want.

4. At some point during your practice take a breather, stop playing. Every pro agrees practicing five hours IN A ROW is a waste of time. Most 'gig' situations revolve around 45 minutes playing, and a 15 minute break. Try that and see how it works. Find some schedule, and then use it. If you are going to have a long practice or rehearsal session, pace yourself.
5. Before you play, scan each exercise for problems or tricky fingering.
6. Think about why you are playing each exercise, and focus your attention on that aspect.
7. Play new exercises slowly ! ! ! ! ! EVERYONE TENDS TO RUSH ALWAYS.
8. After you have mastered an exercise, play it backwards, or with two, three, or four strokes per note. Play the exercises in as many places on the fingerboard as you can. When you understand how, transpose the exercises to other keys. Read everything you can get your hands on.

Be critical and honest with yourself. Give yourself credit for any success you have. If you feel like a loser, you'll have a hard time convincing yourself and others you're not.

Above all, try to enjoy your playing. Accept your errors with ease. Everyone makes mistakes they wish they hadn't. You should not judge yourself any harder than you would others.

Tension and anxiety will add nothing to your playing, so omit them. Relax. When you are unhappy, upset, or irritated by your playing (or your sister), STOP. Then take a long, deep breath, stand up, walk around — do something to help yourself REALLY relax. (Put your sister outside with the cat.) The times now, are too difficult already. You may not be able to enjoy death, famine and destruction, but you SHOULD be able to enjoy your playing (and possibly the cat, if he's outside).

O.K., now that you know what to try and get out of this book, let's get down to the information.

CHAPTER 2

WORDS AND SYMBOLS

This chapter will describe the vocabulary of sound. We will then discuss the kind of sound we hear in music, what makes up this sound, and where to find this sound on the guitar and on paper.

TERMINOLOGY

The following words are used by professional musicians. Make them part of your vocabulary. Good musicianship requires correct words, as well as correct notes.

VIBRATE:

To move back and forth — like a pendulum (or a guitar string).

PITCH:

The rate of vibration of the element producing the sound. A string vibrating at the rate of 440 cycles (a cycle is one complete trip from the beginning, away, and back to the start) per second (C.P.S.) produces the sound we call A. In common usage pitch and note are used interchangeably. Any time you pluck a string in tune, you are creating a pitch. C, D, and E are all pitches. They are also 'notes.'

DURATION:

The length (in time) that a pitch lasts.

QUANTITY:

The volume of the pitch. How loud is it?

QUALITY:

Is the sound sharp? Warm? Piercing? Dark? These are all words that are used to vaguely describe 'quality.' They are inaccurate, and depend for their meanings upon who uses them. Quality is really made up of two kinds of sound, noise and tones. The varying combination of the two parts is what helps make a tuba sound different from a guitar, though they may be playing the same note with the same duration and quantity. What is noise? And what is a tone? Read on . . . .

We are going to divide all the sound we hear into two categories

NOISE:

All sound with irregular vibration. This would include slamming windows, falling rocks, gunshots, and so on.

TONES:

A tone is a sound of a fixed pitch. (Regular vibration.) The sound must be long enough that we may perceive a pitch. Long horn blasts, the repeated ringing of a bell, and the hum of an electric motor are all examples of tones. Of course all musical instruments, and the human voice may also produce tones.* Various instruments create different combinations of tone and noise. Noise, in varying quantities, gives presence to the sound. That is, it makes a clarinet sound 'reedy' and so on.

*Tone has two common usages —

"At the sound of the tone it will be three o'clock." Here tone means a regular sound (as opposed to noise).

"Hey man, I really like the tone of your Fat Bernie guitar. It really has a lot of highs and lows." Here tone is used to mean Quality. Beware of confusion here!! When we mean quality, we will say "TONE QUALITY."

You should be aware of these parts of sound as you listen to music. Do you vary the volume of your playing? Do you use short choppy notes or long sustaining ones? Or both? What about your favorite player? Try the following experiments to hear the parts of your sound, and focus on just the aspect you are testing.

SOUND EXPERIMENT #1

TONE AND QUALITY

Play a chord or single note with your RIGHT HAND close to the neck. Gradually move your right hand away from the neck towards the bridge, and continue strumming. The sound should go from a dark, warm, or mellow sound to a thinner, treble or nasal quality. You are changing the tone quality.

Electric guitars have knobs or switches that can electronically produce a similar change.

SOUND EXPERIMENT #2

DURATION

Play a familiar chord by striking the strings with your right hand and holding your left hand on the chord for a long time, letting the chord die slowly. Then repeat the test, but remove your left hand immediately after you have struck the chord with the right hand. In the first instance you had a long sound, while in the second example you should have had a very brief sound. You are affecting the duration, or length of the sound.

SOUND EXPERIMENT #3

QUANTITY (VOLUME)

Take a familiar song or solo line and vary the volume in different segments. You might start softly and build to a loud ending. Or you might alternate loud and soft in different parts of the song. If you are playing a solo line, try playing one part loudly and then repeating the same part softly, as if it was an echo. Just varying the volume can make a song so much more interesting!

THE GOAL: Understanding these little component parts of musical sound, and being able to manipulate them to suit yourself, will allow you to create tremendous variety and dramatic effects in your playing. It will also help you understand how other players create music that YOU like, and WHY YOU like it. Tone, duration and volume can be manipulated with the same attention and effort that wah-wah, fuzz tone, and other electronic sound changing devices are used. These component parts are more natural, more immediately a part of you, and can be used acoustically or electronically in ANY and ALL styles of music.

Start listening to all the different parts of the band and how different instruments and players use these effects. You will hear many new things you never heard before ! ! ! ! !

The following two words apply to physical distances on the guitar. They will also be used in discussions of harmony and theory later on in this book.

"HALF-STEP":

The distance between any pitch and its closest neighboring pitch. On the guitar moving one fret produces a half step change in pitch.

"WHOLE-STEP":

Two half-steps. Moving two frets on the guitar produces a whole step change.

INTERVAL:

In general, the distance between any two notes. You have a LENGTH of two feet, in the same way that you have an INTERVAL of two half steps, for example.

The word interval is most commonly used when talking about notes in the same scale. We will talk much more about that a little later. For now just use the word to mean 'distance.'

RANGE:

Musically, range is used to mean "a group of NOTES". "Her voice had a wide range." This means she could sing high and low notes—or "She had a strong high range"—her upper notes were clear and loud.

NOTATION (SYMBOLS)

This section is more "head work." It deals with putting the music down on paper. Go slowly and read everything very carefully. If you do not understand this fully, everything that follows will be more confusing.

Music is notated on a staff (plural staves) composed of lines and spaces. Notes may appear on a line or on a space. There are five lines and four spaces. The lines and spaces are always counted from the bottom upwards.

The Staff	Note on 1st line	Note on 1st space

9

Horizontally the staff is divided into spaces called measures, by vertical lines called bar lines. How many notes can be in a measure? Our chapter on time answers that completely.

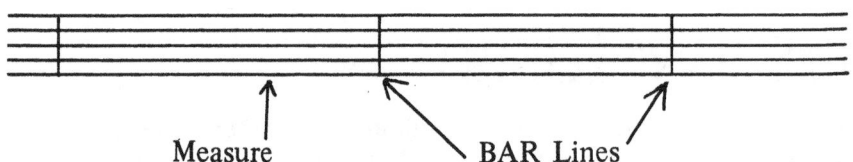

Measure   BAR Lines

THE NOTES

We have more pitches than note names. So rather than create more names, and to help keep it organized, we repeat the names. We use the first seven letters of the alphabet – A B C D E F G. The names were given to notes in an ascending order. That is, B is higher than the A next to it, and D is higher than C, and so on.

A_1 B_1 C D E F G A_2 B_2 C D E F G   A B C D E F G   A   etc.
Low ————————————————————————————→ High

However, because we repeat the names of the notes over and over as we go higher and higher in pitch, you can see that there is a situation when an A note would be 'higher' than a B note. (A_2 is higher in pitch than B_1.) There is no problem here, though, because when we write the notes on the staff, we fix each one to one place only. And A_2 is nowhere near A_1. As the notes ascend in pitch, they also get higher on the staff. In the example below, the first note is higher than the second.

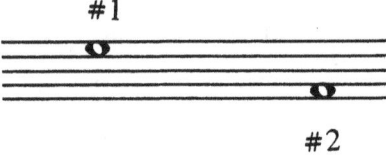

THE CLEF:

The clef sign determines the names of the notes on the staff. While there are several different clefs in use today, we will need only the most common one, the G clef (so called because the curl in the sign circles the line on which the G note appears). Because the G note is positioned on the second line, all the other notes will appear on the staff according to their position in the alphabet. We need the clef to tell us this though, because the G note can be written in other places for other instruments. The bass guitar, because of its low sound, has a different clef, and the G note is on the top space.

G Clef   F Clef or "Bass Clef"

For now concern yourself with the G clef. Most of the time this is the only clef you will see.

Because there are more pitches than will fit on a staff, extra lines called ledger lines may be added above or below the staff.

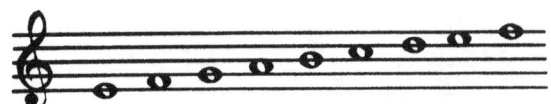

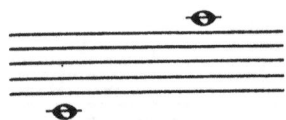

The notes placed on the staff.   LEDGER lines with NOTES

Essentially music on paper is a code system. Where the dots (notes) appear vertically on the paper will determine which fret and string you will play. The color, shape and size of the note will determine when you will play it, and how long you will sustain the note.

Since we are going to start with reading the notes only, and not immediately deal with how long and when to play them, we will use a big, easy to read note, the "whole note."

In the opening examples, play each whole note with equal volume, duration, and tone. Play the notes at an even pace. Do not slow down and speed up at will, but try to imitate the smooth, even ticking of a clock.**

How fast should you play your smooth, even "ticking"? VERY SLOWLY ! ! ! ! ! Play slowly enough that you make NO mistakes by the third or fourth time you play a new example. At the start this will seem like an eternity, but don't despair! This slow stage will pass very quickly.

If you rush or skip exercises, you'll find later that you will not be able to read quickly, so do everything carefully. As you practice you will find that you will reach a point where you begin to make MANY mistakes. Just stop, take a breather and then return to the trouble spot and play it at a slower pace. This situation will occur frequently even as you become professional and accomplished at reading and playing, so remember the solution!

**It sometimes helps in establishing the speed, to count out loud, or tap out loud or . . ., at least four counts before you begin. This gives you a chance to hear the pulse before you have to jump in and play right along. This is done very commonly by professionals. You can often hear them counting off before a song, "1, 2, 3, 4."

NOTATION (CONTINUED)

Below is the treble clef and the notes as they appear on the lines and spaces.

MEMORIZE THESE NOTES.

Lines   Spaces

Every Good Boy Does Fine   F A C E

Identify the following notes.
Practice recognizing the notes until you really KNOW their names.

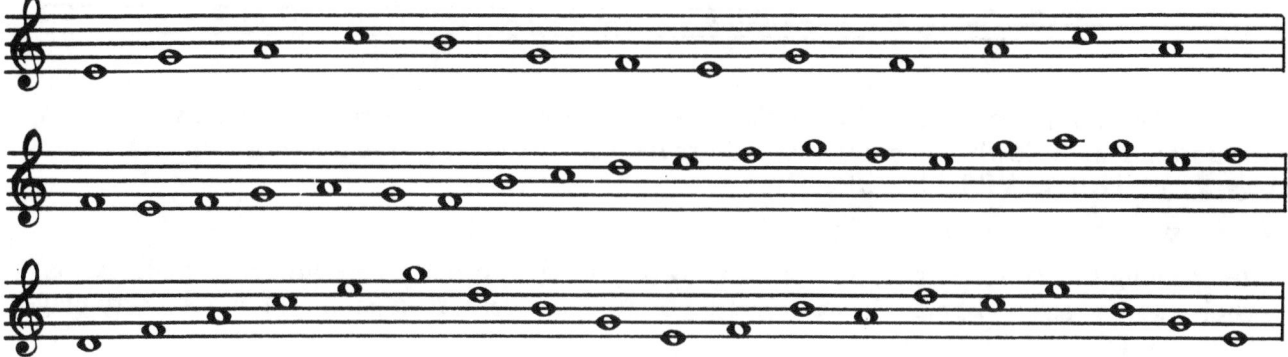

CHAPTER 3

O.K. . . . It's time to get out your guitar.

We are now ready to learn the notes on the first three frets. The diagram below shows the notes of the first string and their location on the guitar. An 'O' means to play the string open — without pressing on a fret.

The First String

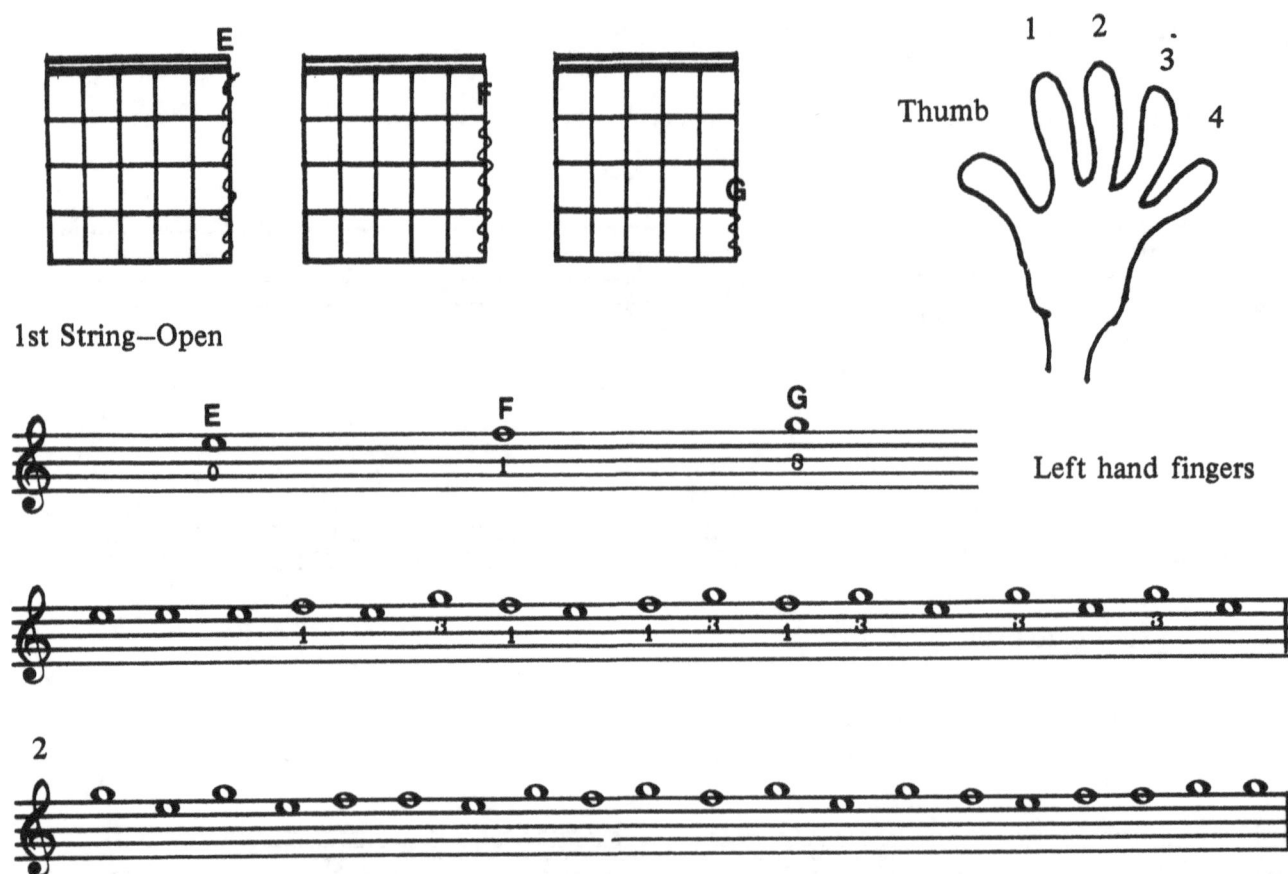

1st String—Open

Left hand fingers

Identify the note names of ex. 1, then play the exercise with the fingers indicated, without naming the notes. Play it slowly and evenly. Use alternate picking (down on the first note, up on the second ♦ ♦) THIS IS VERY IMPORTANT!

Do not stop to replay an error. Continue on.

After playing the exercise once, go back, and with your eye, check where you stumbled. Replay the whole exercise again. Replay the exercise till you feel confident, then go on. (You might try playing it right to left, just for fun.)

THE SECOND STRING

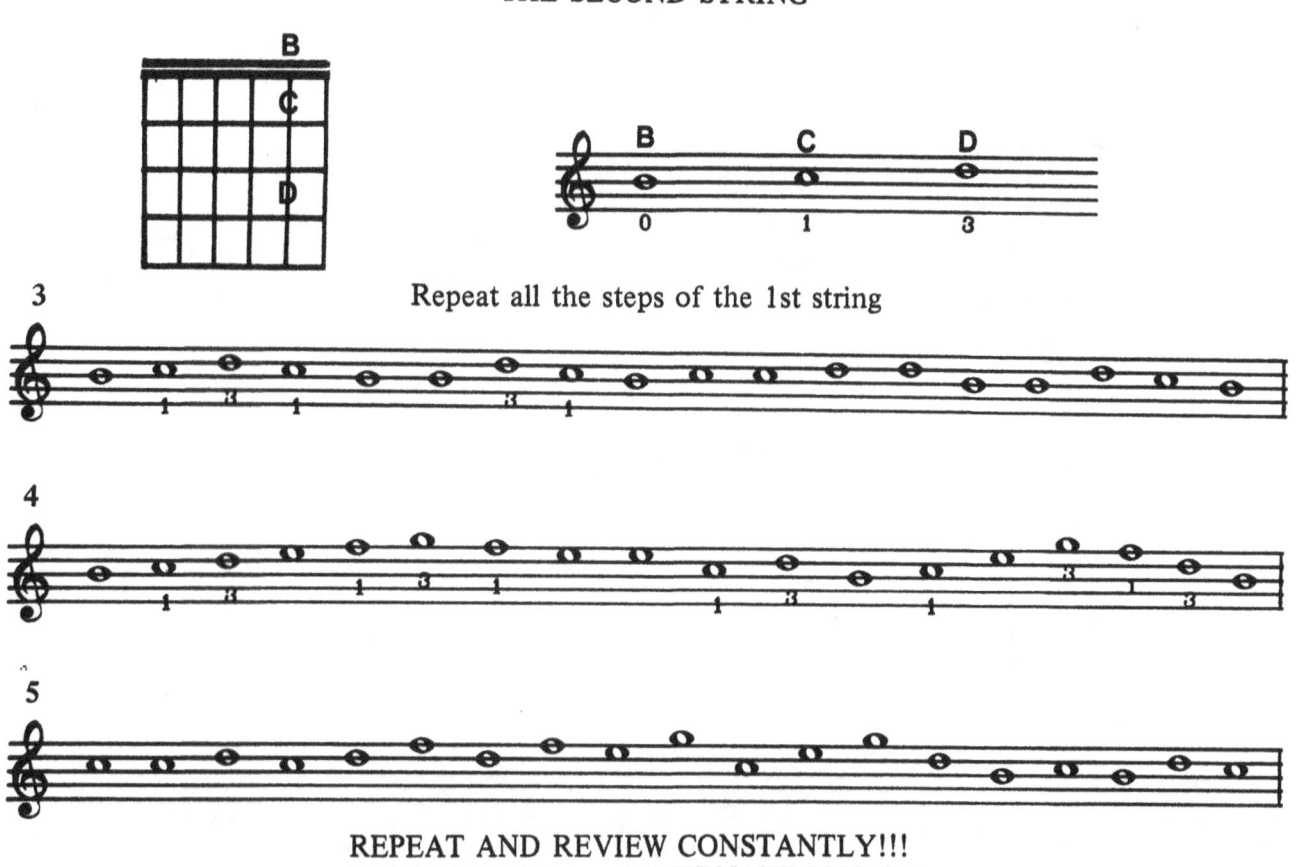

3

Repeat all the steps of the 1st string

4

5

REPEAT AND REVIEW CONSTANTLY!!!
DON'T FORGET – ALTERNATE PICKING

THE THIRD STRING

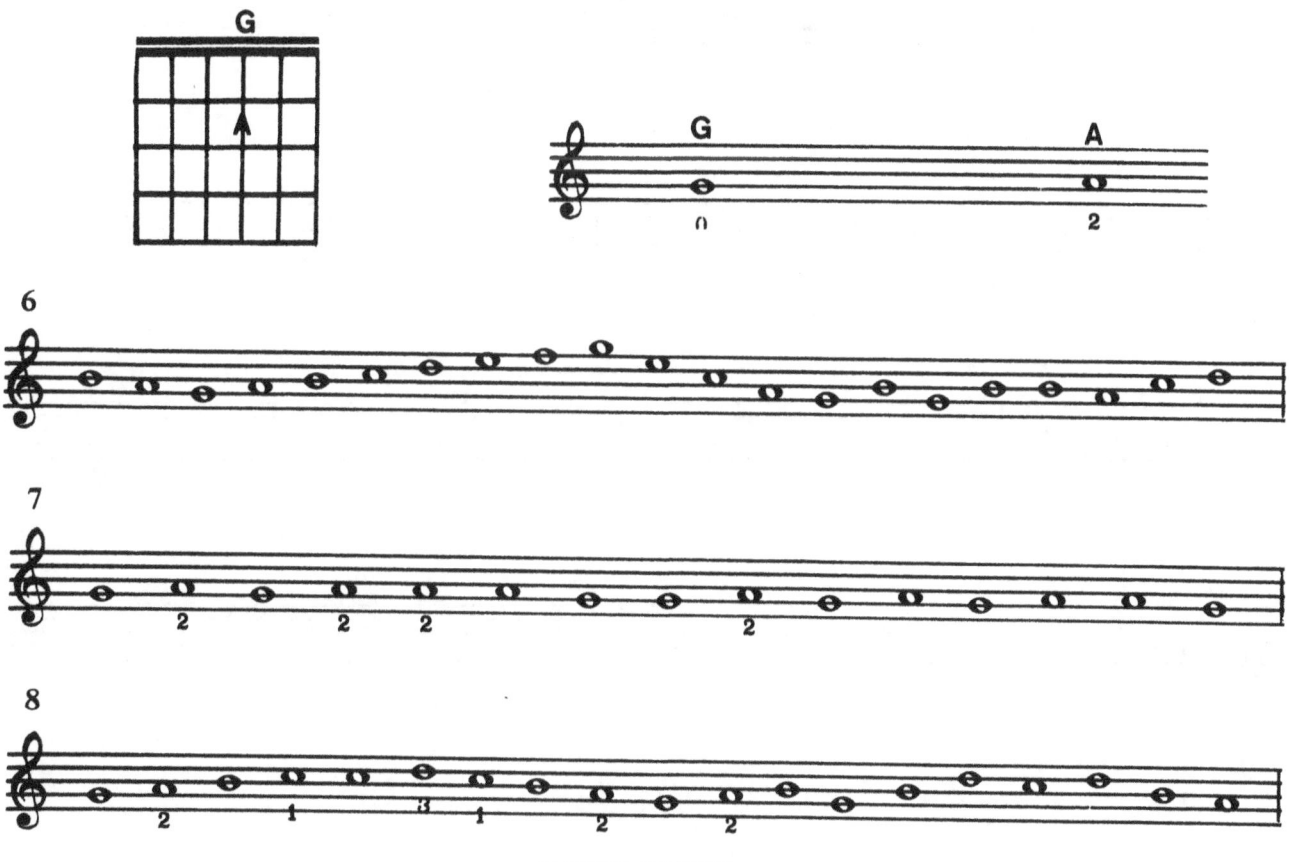

6

7

8

DON'T RUSH!

THE FOURTH STRING

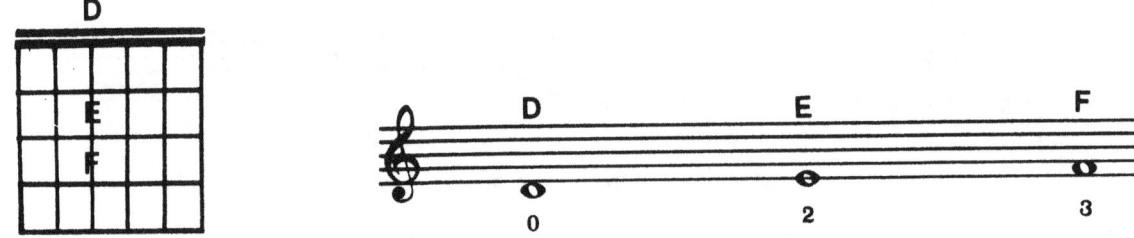

Continue as before. Practice naming the notes, then play.

9

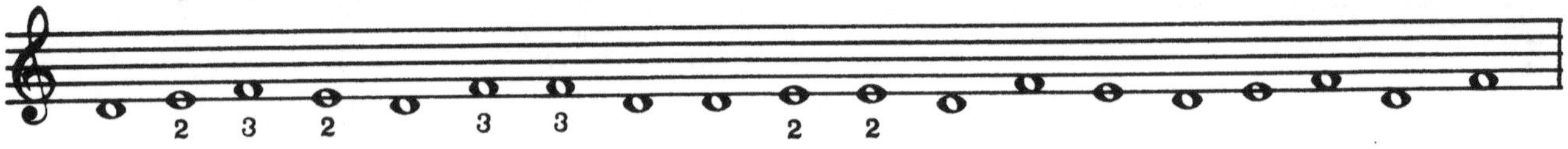

10

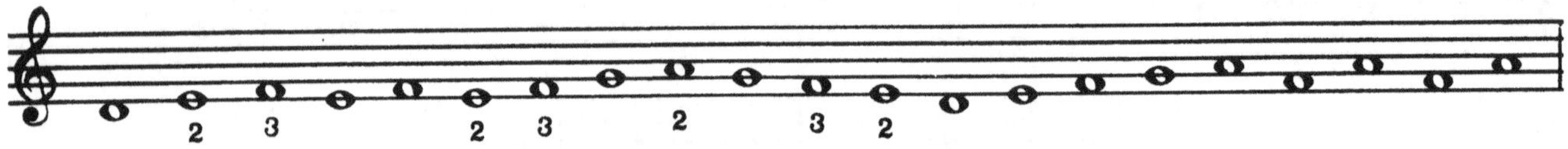

11

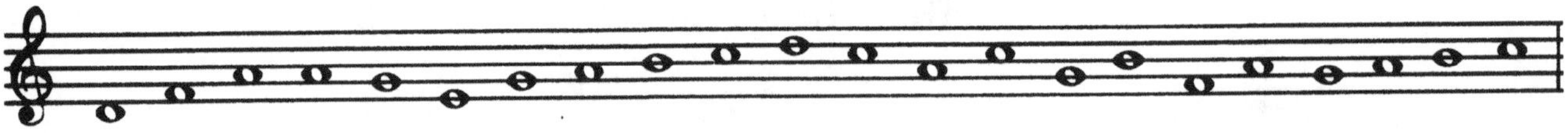

12

13

14

Play the exercises above from right to left —
It's good for your eye.

THE FIFTH STRING

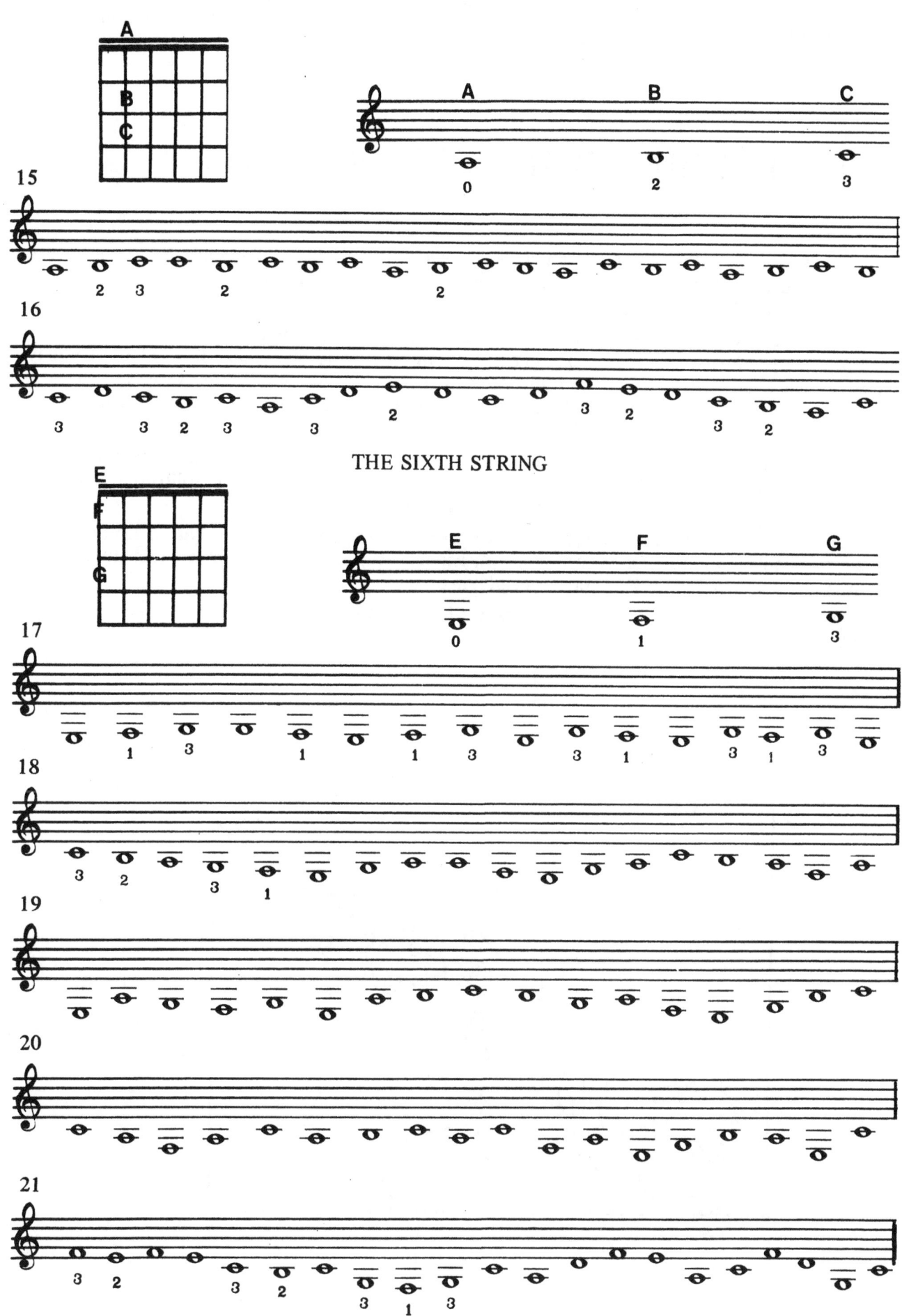

THE SIXTH STRING

Before continuing on, be SURE you can play ALL the notes. It would be a good idea to replay all the exercises without stopping, just to check yourself. You should be able to play them at a moderate speed. (On the metronome, set at 80, or ♩ = 80 up to 144 — with each note getting one tick.)

THE METRONOME: THE WHAAT? . . . . .

Everyone is familiar with the ticking of a clock. It is regular, and even. If a clock ticked once every second, it would tick 60 times a minute. If we had an accelerator, like you find on a car, connected to our clock, we could speed it up or slow it down at our will.

This is a metronome. The metronome provides a 'ticker' which can be controlled to tick slowly or fast, or any degree in between. Musicians use the metronome to help them control how fast they play the music. There are two kinds of metronomes, which both do the same thing. One is a wind-up, mechanical spring type mechanism which can be used anywhere. The newer variety of metronome is the electric kind.

Once we progress into the rhythm section of the book, you will see how the metronome may be used in more advanced study. For now if you wish to use a metronome, do the following: play one note (we are using the whole note) for each tick you hear.

You may find that the constant ticking can begin to bug you after a while. That is normal. The best way to handle a metronome is to turn it on, listen to the speed you have set, then turn it off, count off your music ("1 2 3 4") and begin playing.

If you wish to speed up the music, stop, turn on the metronome, listen to the new speed you set, then turn it off and begin again at that new speed.

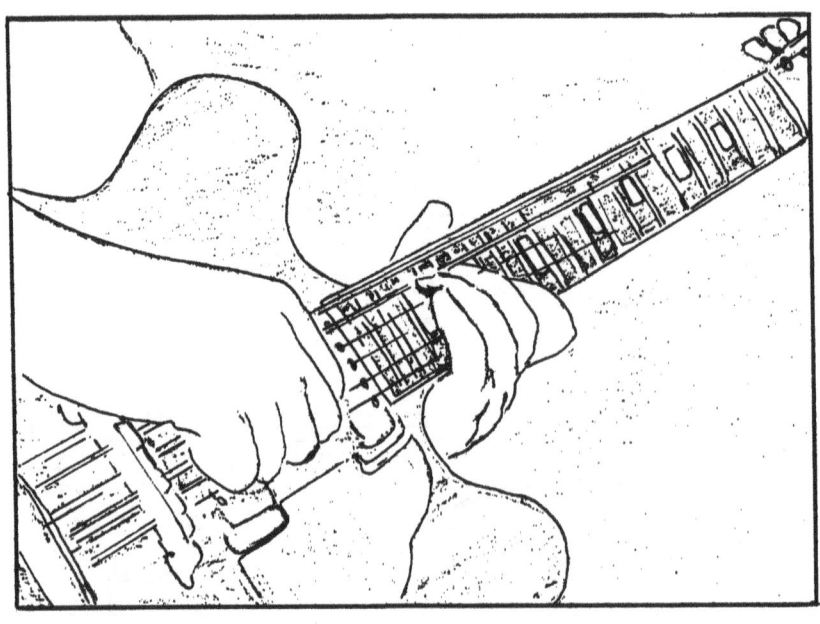

CHAPTER 4

NOTES, NOTES, NOTES!

Many wind instruments and the piano have only one way of playing each note on their instruments. That is, 'middle C' can be found in only one place on the piano keyboard. And on trumpets, clarinets and so on there is only one combination of fingers and lips that will let the player make the note 'middle C.'

The guitar, however, is blessed with a different system of making sound. Because there are strings, which may be tuned to whatever notes a player may want, it is possible to find a note like 'middle C' in more than one place on the neck.

The system of tuning the guitar which is most commonly used, was developed through hundreds of years of trial and error efforts to find a way to play more than one note at the same time, easily. So, we are now able to play many notes in as many as five (!) different places on the guitar!!

DON'T PANIC?! This is an advantage, and there is no confusion in making a choice of which 'middle C' you want to play. Your hand is only so big, with a certain limit to how much stretching, groping, and straining you can do. Because there is more than one place to play any one note, you can pick and choose the most comfortable and easy location.

Below is a picture of the first five frets of the guitar, with notes that can be played in two places indicated.

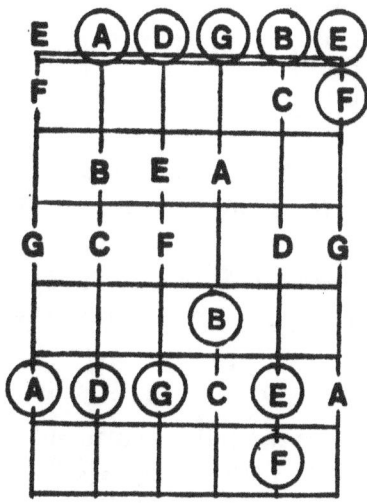

The pitches on the staff

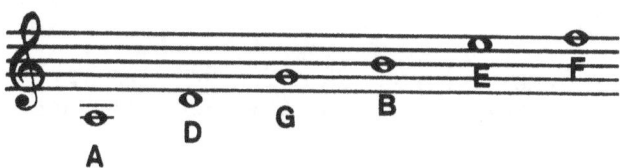

In fact, there are convenient patterns and groups of notes on the guitar that actually AID YOU in sight reading!

There are also straight forward, logical rules which you will follow to determine which pattern or general location you will use to read and play.

POSITION PLAYING

Below is the first of eight fingering patterns that we will use in our reading. They are easy to remember because they are very similar to each other.

Pay close attention to where your fingers are supposed to go, and memorize this pattern so that you can play it without looking at your guitar.

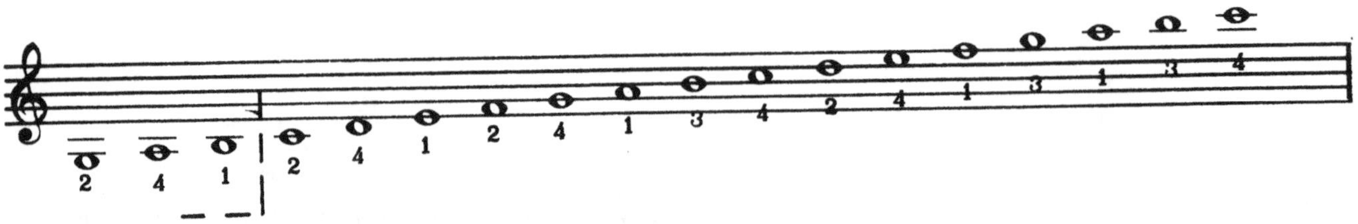

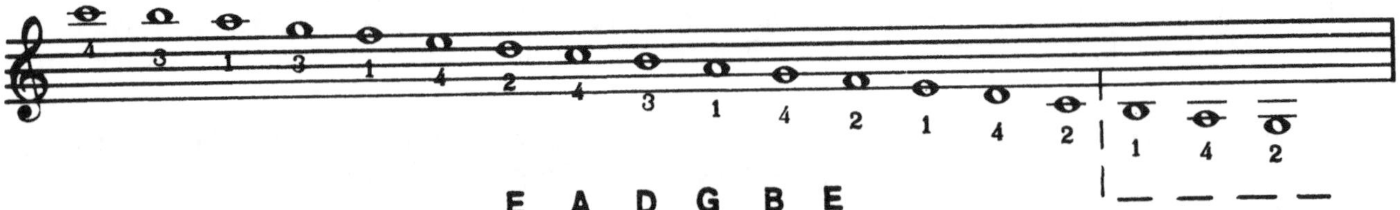

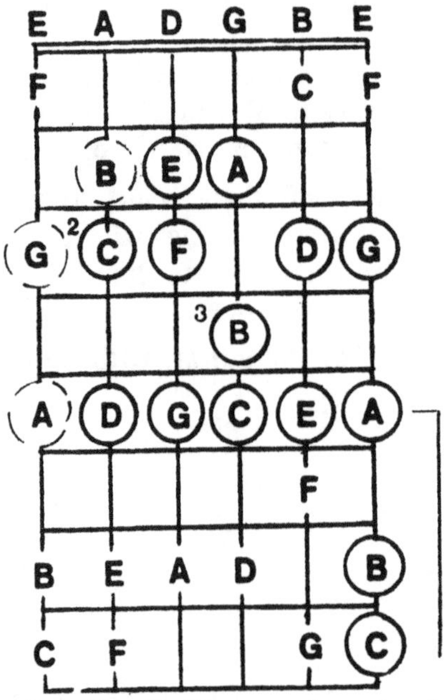

This pattern has a name. We call it "2a." The number stands for the finger of your left hand that the pattern starts on. The letter is the name of the string which the pattern begins on (here, the A string).

In this pattern you will notice that you are able to play all the notes you already know, plus a new group of three higher notes, A, B, and C. Playing these notes requires you to move your hand, but this is a simple movement.

As you can see, reaching for low F requires a slight stretch also.

Go back and practice all your exercises in this new position. Say the letter names out loud or use any aid you can think of to help yourself learn the new positions of these notes. HOWEVER, once this pattern is familiar to you through TOUCH, you must stop looking at your guitar!!! That is most important. Keep your eyes on the page. Go slowly, and use alternate picking.

If you feel unsure of your right hand picking, practice the exercise below. It is also good for learning this new 2a pattern.

22

Play each note of 2a two times. Once with a down stroke, and once with an up stroke.

Play the following exercises in your new position, 2a.
DON'T RUSH — WORK SLOWLY AND CAREFULLY!
USE ALTERNATE PICKING.

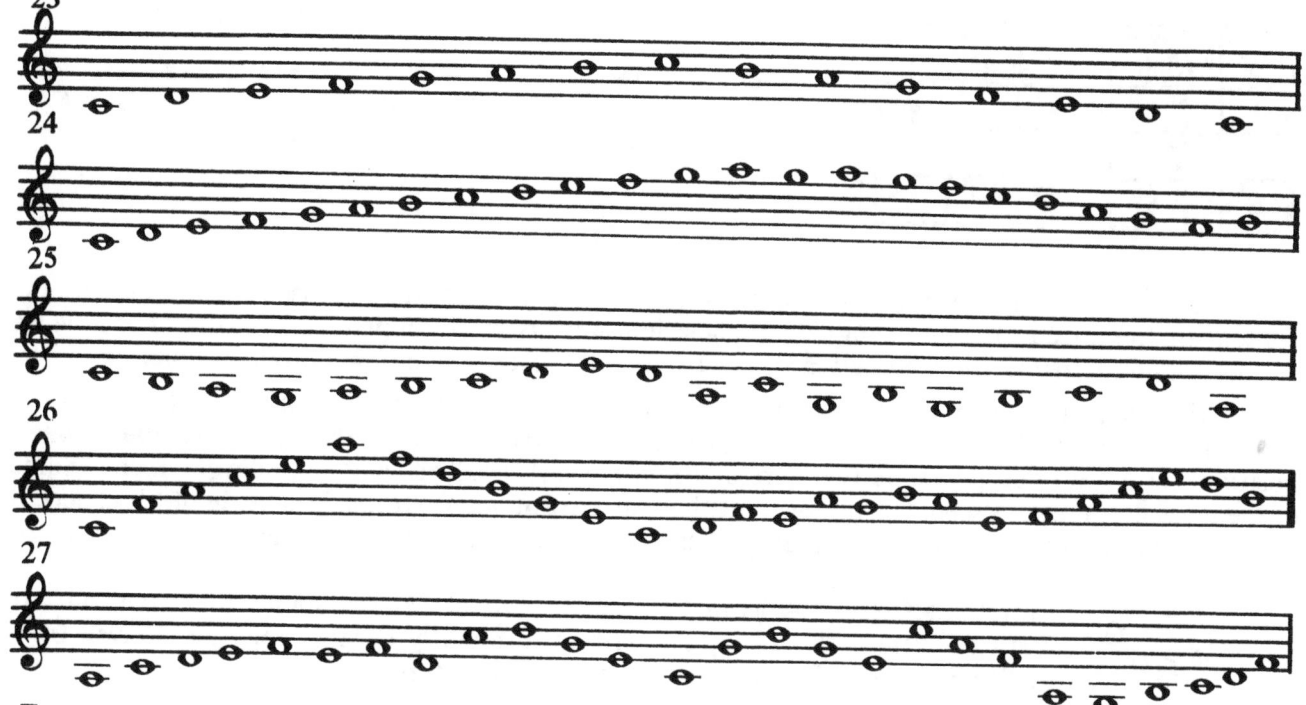

Try these exercises right to left!

So far we have learned these notes: C   D   E   F   G   A   B
Now we will introduce the rest of our notes, and the signs that help make their names.

\# — That sign is the 'sharp.' It appears on the staff like a note.

When you see this sign, you RAISE the note it appears in front of, by one half step (one fret).

GUITAR
FINGERBOARD

b — This sign is called the 'flat.' It appears on the staff like a note, also when you see it in front of a note, play that note one half step lower.

Say, doesn't that note between F and G
have two names?   Yes, READ ON . . .

Using these two signs we may find the rest of our notes. Below is a diagram of the new notes, as they occur in our musical alphabet.

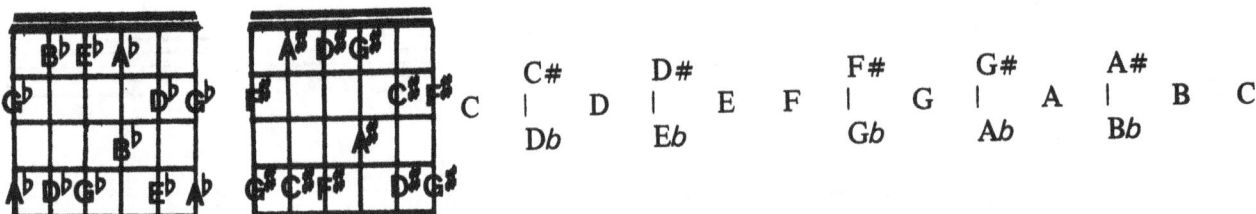

You'll see that these new notes have two names. Which name and sign you use is determined by the context of the music. A more complete explanation appears in the appendix on scales. For now we will use only one name for each new note, and you will see only one new note at a time.

It is important to understand that these new notes are named according to their position. That is, F# is one fret above F. And Gb is one fret lower than G. Also remember that the notes, their names, positions, and the rules governing them are a product of historical trial and error development. Some of the ideas don't always seem useful now, but they are part of what our music is made of. Just accept them as best you can, and use only what applies now to your particular learning level.

ENHARMONIC: A word to describe two tones that sound the same, but are written differently. They are written differently because they are derived from different tones. F# and Gb are 'enharmonic' tones.

Sharps and flats are used in music in two different ways. They're commonly known as accidentals.

1. **'Accidentally'**: A sharp or flat may be introduced into the music temporarily. That is, the composer wants that note changed up or down one fret for just a little while. The sharp or flat affects the note only for the measure it appears in. In the next measure, the note returns to its original pitch.

The notes in measures
1 and 3 are the same —
The note in measure 2
is one fret higher.

The notes in measures
1 and 3 are the same pitch.
The note in measure 2 is
one fret lower.

The natural ♮ ; the natural is a third sign that is employed to return a sharped or flatted pitch back to its regular pitch before the end of the measure.

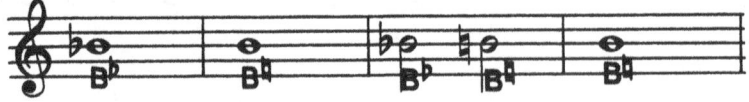

2. **On purpose**: If a composer wants a note to be played sharped or flatted all the way through the piece of music, he puts it at the beginning of the music. Then every time you see that note you play it up one fret (unless it is preceded by the 'natural').

20

We are now going to introduce our second pattern, which is very closely related to our 2a pattern. In fact, all the notes in this new pattern are the same, except one. Instead of F, we will play F#. This position is called 2e.

Learn the new fingering, and then proceed to the following exercises.

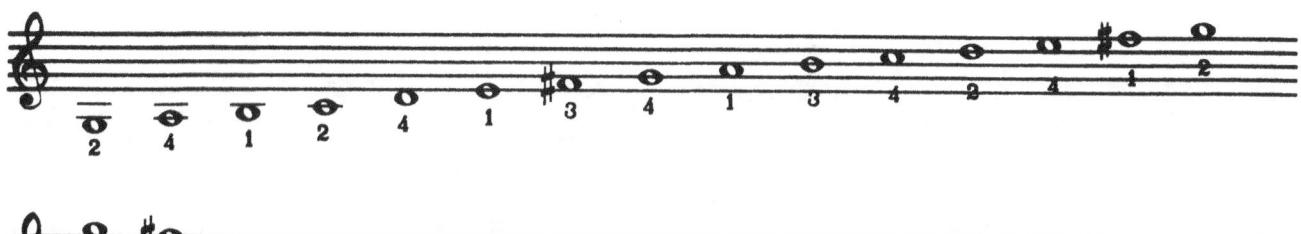

Repeat the two lines above until memorized by touch.

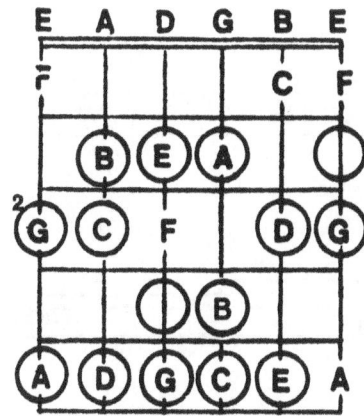

PATTERN 2e

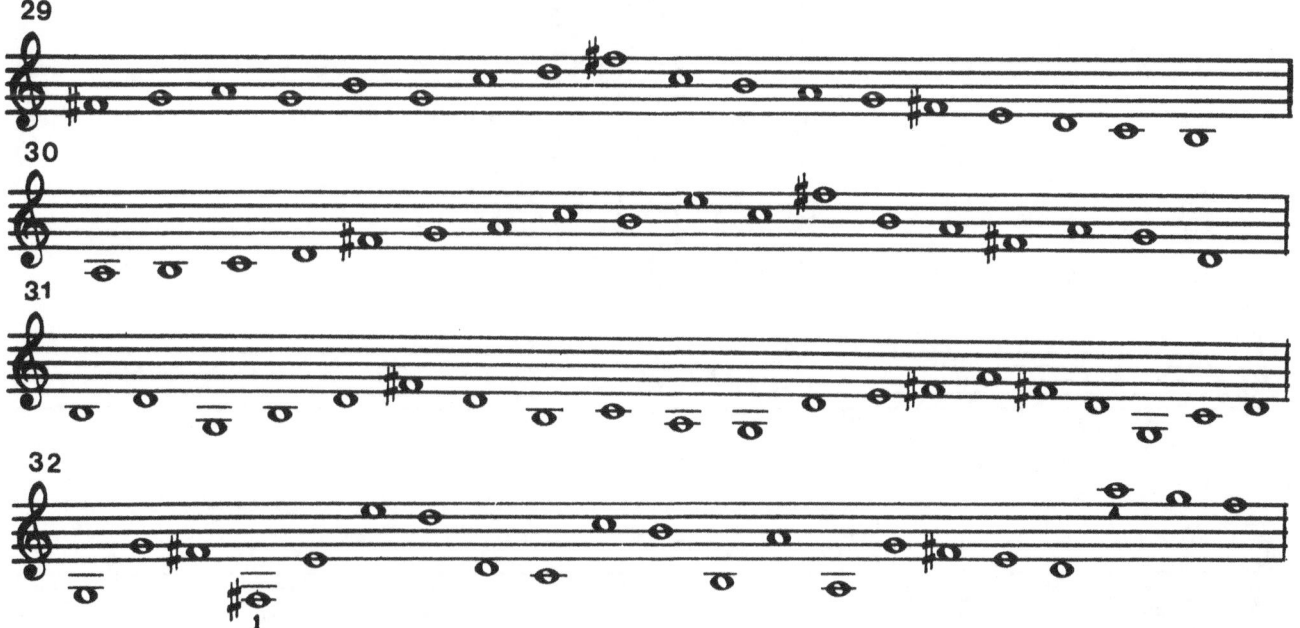

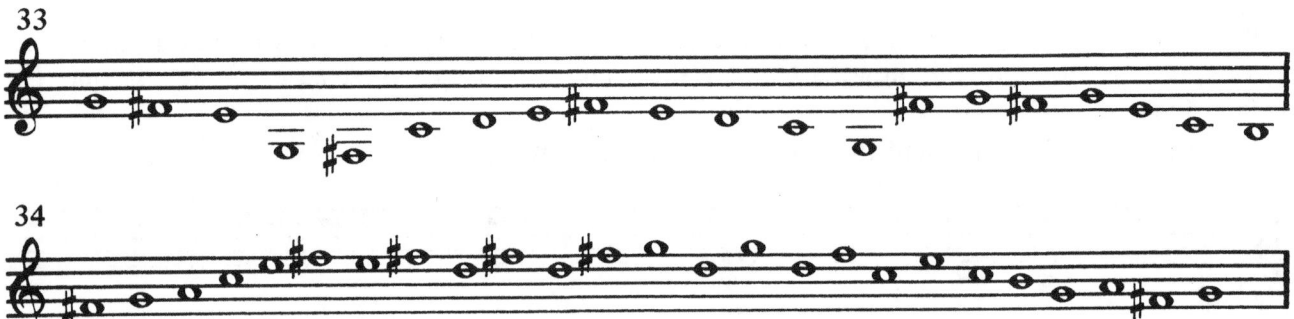

Now that you have had some experience with patterns beginning with your second finger, we will introduce a brand new kind of pattern. This pattern begins with your fourth finger, and we are going to jump way down to the eighth fret to learn it.

DON'T PANIC! This fingering is comfortable . . . There are NO new notes . . . You will have seen two-thirds of the neck, when you have completed this section of the book.

The pattern is shown below. It starts on your fourth finger, on the eighth fret on the bass E string. The name of the pattern is 4e.

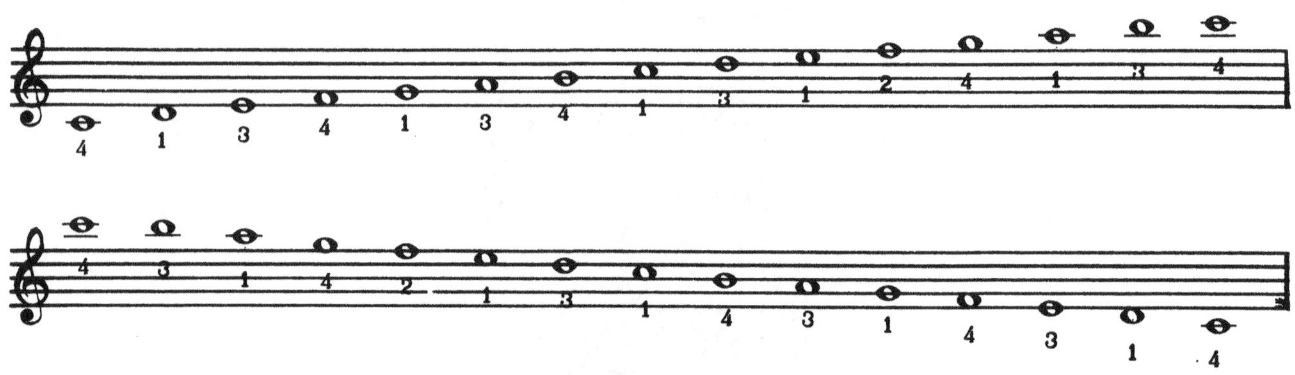

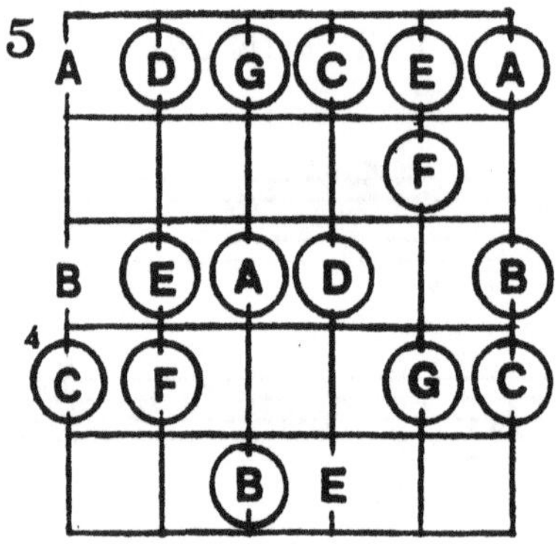

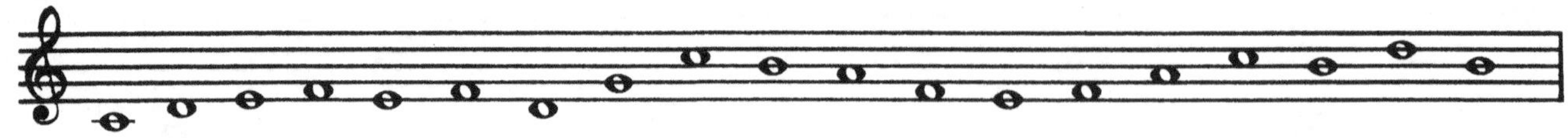

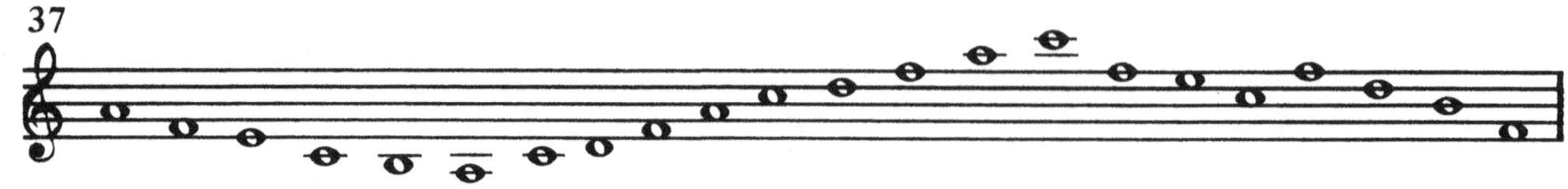

CHAPTER 5

HEAD WORK

This chapter contains the "meat and potatoes" of our whole musical system, and how it works on the guitar.

Before you continue on, you should read the section hidden at the back of the book called, "Appendix on the Derivation of Scales." There is a great amount of useful background information there that should fill in the gaps of most players at this stage of their learning. It has Romance! Adventure! Science! and History! Not to mention an all star cast including Miriam the wonder goose! Actually, it contains information on our scales, notes, how they were developed in the ancient world, and how science, musicians, and time evolved all of this into what we play today. Please at least glance through it before continuing on to this chapter.

SCALES

If you have not yet read the appendix on the derivation of our musical scales, you should do so now before continuing. A brief summary shows that —

1. Our ancestors created groups of notes in certain patterns.
2. These groups most commonly had eight notes in them.
3. These notes were organized in a specific order, with each note being a predetermined distance from its neighbor notes.
4. These groups correspond to what we call scales.

What is a scale?

SCALE:

A succession of pitches in a fixed order. There may be any number in any order of descension or ascension. (This means that you can have scales in which the notes are above and below the note you start on, rather than progressing upwards only or downwards only.) For example —

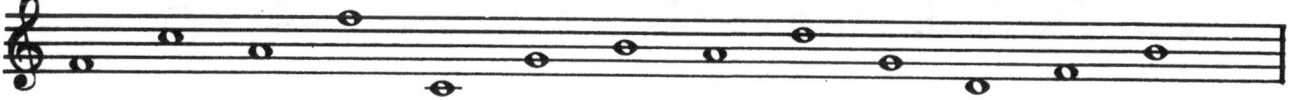

Above is a group of notes in a fixed order (because we find them there) — a scale. It is a random pattern, and of no practical use, but it does qualify as a scale.

DIATONIC:

The name of a scale with eight notes, arranged in a particular whole step, half step order (shown below). This is the only grouping known as "DIATONIC."

DIATONIC SCALE   W = Whole Step   3–4   7–8 are half steps

EL 2786

The three patterns you have learned so far have been diatonic eight-note scales (repeated twice cdefgabc, defgabc). Because a scale has a formula function (i.e., it determines the distances between notes) a scale can be started on any note.

Our 2a, and 4e patterns are C scales. The 2e pattern is a G scale.

```
C   D   E   F   G   A   B   C
            C scale  1 octave

G   A   B   C   D   E   F#  G
            G scale  1 octave
```

*OCTAVE:

(from octo meaning 8). The distance between the first and eighth note of an eight note diatonic scale. Also the distance from any letter name note to the next time the note is seen.

In the Western culture, much of our music is based on these scales; our melodies and chords are derived from these scales. When a composer writes music based on the C scale, and since we have several places on the guitar where we can find the scale and any of the notes in it, it becomes easy to read the notes of this composer's piece. That is why we learn scales. IN ADDITION — If you take a scale and combine the notes in it to form chords (a chord being two or more notes played at once), you will see that most of our musical chord changes, and movement from chord to chord, occur within a single scale.

For example —

How many songs do you know with some of these chords? C, F, G, or C, Aminor, Dminor, G, or Dminor, G, C. There are thousands of songs with these changes.

When you move from note to note, you are dealing with a scale. When you move from chord to chord, and these chords are made up of notes in the SAME scale, you are dealing with KEY.

KEY:

A key is a family or group of tones all in one major diatonic scale. The idea of key includes both single notes and notes struck in groups (chords).

As we have seen, there is only one scale which contains no notes with sharps or flats. That is the C major* scale. Every other scale contains sharped or flatted notes. How can we remember which scales have which sharps or flats???

At the beginning of every piece of music is a 'KEY SIGNATURE.'

*For a discussion of "MAJOR" see appendix on scales.

KEY SIGNATURES:

At the beginning of a musical composition there is a sign that tells you if you will have to play any sharps or flats in the piece. It is called the key signature.

It is composed of the G clef and sharp or flat signs. A sharp or flat sign, whenever it is used in music, appears on the same line or space as the note it affects. For example —

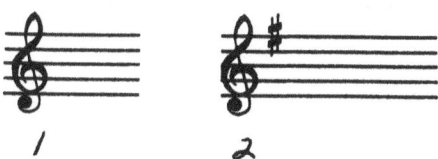

In key signature #1 there are no sharps or flats, so you would play the seven regular notes you already know. In ex. #2 there is a sharp sign appearing on the line where the F note is placed. So any time ANY F note is to be played in the music with this key signature, you play F sharp instead.

(Except if a natural sign is used. Then you'd play F)

Note — In key signatures you will see either sharps or flats but never BOTH!*

*Sometimes a composer will combine sharps and flats in a Key Signature to call your attention to it. For instance, if he is CHANGING keys. But this is not the norm.

We have learned positions for scales, which contain all the notes in a key. The key signature tells us which key we are in, and therefore which scale to play. The position that we choose for that scale depends on where the highest and lowest notes are in the music.

This is how this works —
If you see a key signature at the beginning of a song, with no sharps or flats, which key are you in? The answer is C. Therefore whatever finger position you choose, it should begin on a C note. If it does, then you will be able to play all the notes in a C SCALE, and so in the KEY of C. Which position you choose will be determined by your own taste and which notes you have to play. If you have many high notes, then a position focusing there would be better than one which is only comfortable to you for lower notes. To begin with, the positions will be given to you, so don't worry about getting lost. (NOTE: Please memorize the key signatures in the appendix on scales and keys. This is CRITICAL!!)

Build scales on the following notes. Make the scales eight note diatonic scales. Each scale can have only one note with a particular letter name. (No scale should have, for example, F AND F#, or D AND D♭.)

To build the scale, begin on the first note and count up the correct number of half steps or whole steps to each of the notes. A piano keyboard is shown below for reference. Scales will have either sharps or flats, but NO scale will have both!

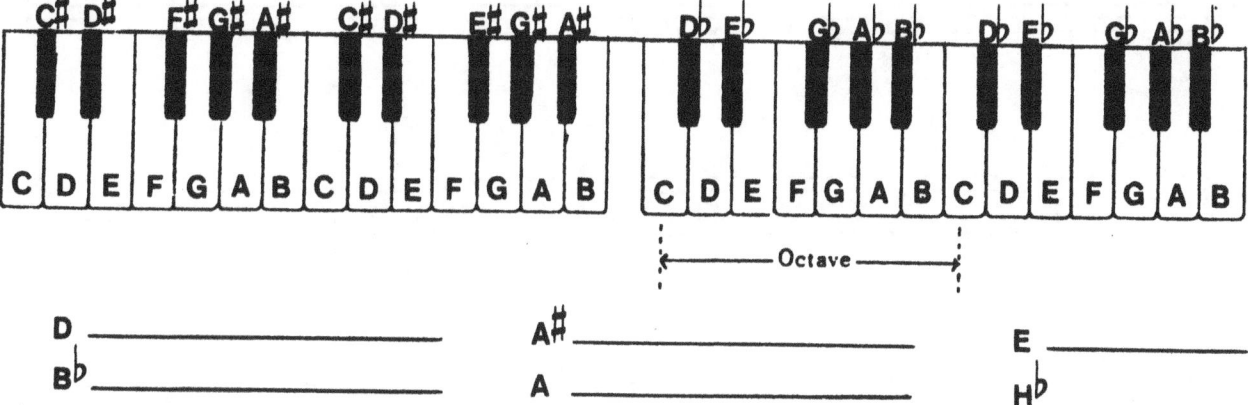

D _____   A♯ _____   E _____

B♭ _____   A _____   H♭

POSITION EXERCISES

Scale fingering 2e is a G major scale. The key of G major (and the G major scale), have one note which is sharped—f#. This appears in the key signature. Scale fingering 2a is a C major scale. The key of C major, and the C major scale have no sharp or flat notes, and so there are no sharps or flats in the key signature. By looking at the key signature for each of the following exercises figure out which scale fingering you should use, 2a or 2e.

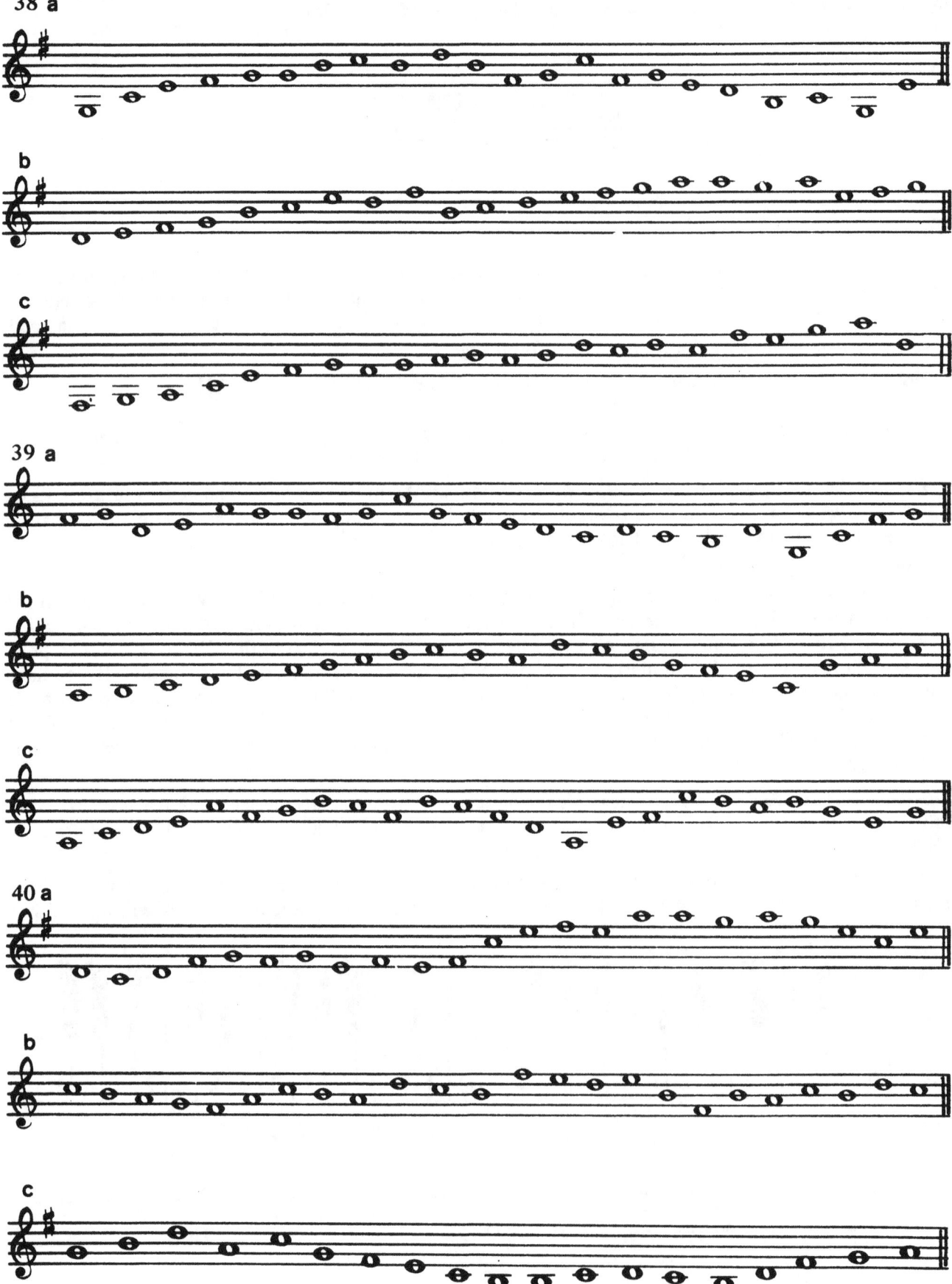

CHAPTER 6

TIME

Until now we have been concerned with WHERE the different notes can be found on the guitar, and WHERE they are located on paper. We have been seeing only one kind of note, the whole note. We have not discussed notes of different length in time.

We will now take up this discussion.

Before we hop right into the ideas about WHEN to play, we must first get some more vocabulary and some new notation.

Discussions and concepts of time and rhythm in music can be very confusing, yet good playing depends on understanding what happens WHEN, and WHY.

BEAT:

A throb in music — it can be a clap, tap (or 'throb,' and not necessarily sounded).

PULSE:

A regular symmetrical beat.

A single tick of a clock could be called a BEAT. It could occur once, or more than once. The constant, repeated ticking of the clock represents the idea of PULSE.

TEMPO:

A musical word meaning speed. You have the 'speed of the plane,' and the 'tempo of the music.' The only way to measure tempo is if there are regular even pulses, like the ticking of our clock. The faster the tick, or pulse, the faster the tempo.

New notation:

As we have said: Horizontally the staff is divided into spaces called MEASURES, by vertical lines called BAR LINES.

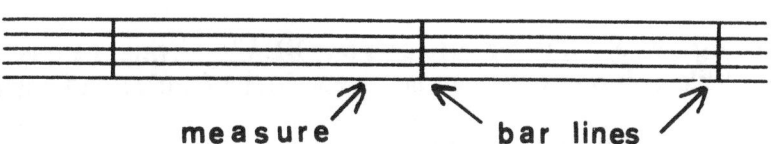

The note is the dot that is placed on paper to indicate which musical pitch we are to play, how long and when we are to play it. The position of the note on the staff (vertically) determines the pitch. The duration is shown by the color and construction of the note.

| WHOLE NOTE | HALF NOTE | QUARTER NOTE | EIGHTH NOTE |

27

In our history, a complete measure of music was considered to have four beats. This four beats was represented by a complete circle. It had a value of "one" in that it was one complete unit. So our other notes that were parts of the measure came to be called according to their fractional part of the completed measure, or "one." So a note that was two beats or half the measure was a 'half note.' And a quarter note was one-fourth of a measure of four beats, or one beat.

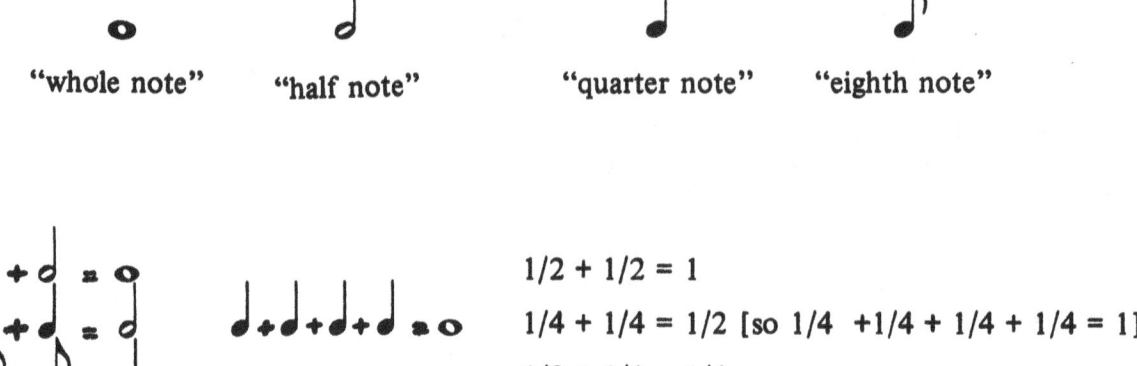

"whole note"   "half note"   "quarter note"   "eighth note"

$$1/2 + 1/2 = 1$$

$$1/4 + 1/4 = 1/2 \text{ [so } 1/4 + 1/4 + 1/4 + 1/4 = 1]$$

$$1/8 + 1/8 = 1/4$$

$$1/8 + 1/8 = 1/4$$

[also 1/8th notes]

RESTS

Rests are like notes. They have a definite way of being written, they have specific time values, and they appear in music as frequently. The big difference is that rests indicate silence rather than sound. Below are the rests equal to the notes we know.

whole rest   half rest   quarter rest   eighth rest

In music with the $\frac{4}{4}$ time signature, a quarter note gets one BEAT. Giving the quarter note one beat is very common, and the table below shows comparative values of notes and rests in this system.

4 beats	whole note	o	A whole rest	▬
2 beats	half note	𝅗𝅥	A half rest	▬
1 beat	quarter note	♩	A quarter rest	𝄽
½ beat	eighth note	♪	An eighth rest	𝄾

Each measure of music has a certain number of beats in it. How many beats, and how many beats of WHAT KIND OF NOTE, is determined by a sign at the beginning of the music called a Time signature.

The time signature is written as one number above another number. $\frac{4}{4}$ is a time signature.

The bottom number tells you what kind of note gets one beat.

The top number tells you how many beats there will be in a measure.

4 . . . 4 beats per measure
4 . . . 1/4 note gets 1 beat . . . so

Whatever the time signature says, MUST BE contained in each measure. The number of beats in a measure can be made up of any combination of notes and rests, as long as there is the correct number of beats. Below is an example of $\frac{4}{4}$ measures, with different rests and notes.

Study this example carefully!!

PICK-UP NOTES

There is one occasion when you may see fewer notes than there should be, in a bar. At the beginning of a song, if the melody begins in the middle of a bar, often it will be written in just that way. Usually the extra notes are picked up at the end of that section of music.

These double bars, and double dots mean to repeat the music in between them, once, after you've played it the first time

TIME SIGNATURES: PRACTICE EXERCISES

Following are some examples of correct time signatures. Analyze each one and write the correct description following the signature.

4 **4**	**3** **8**
3 **4**	**7** **8**
6 **4**	**5** **8**
3 **2**	**4** **8**
2 **2**	**6** **8**

If you have $\frac{4}{4}$ time, and you have four quarter notes in a measure, then each note gets one beat — and gets ALL of that beat. However, it is possible to divide the beat up into smaller parts.

If , then in a bar of $\frac{4}{4}$ you could have two eighth notes for every quarter note.

How would you play these?

To divide the beat up and count it out loud we would say, "One and, Two and, Three and, Four and." The first half of the beat is the "one," and the second half of the beat is the "and."

"1 and   2 and   3 and   4 and"

*Eighth notes are written two ways. If an eighth note is the only note being played in a beat, it has a little flag (example A). If the eighth is being played with some other note IN THE beat, then it is connected with a beam (example B).

If a measure of music is ALL eighth notes, it may be written as in example C.

Below are some examples of notes in correctly written musical situations. Count them all out loud, and understand where the notes are played. Then play the examples.

RHYTHM PRACTICE

Fill in the blanks

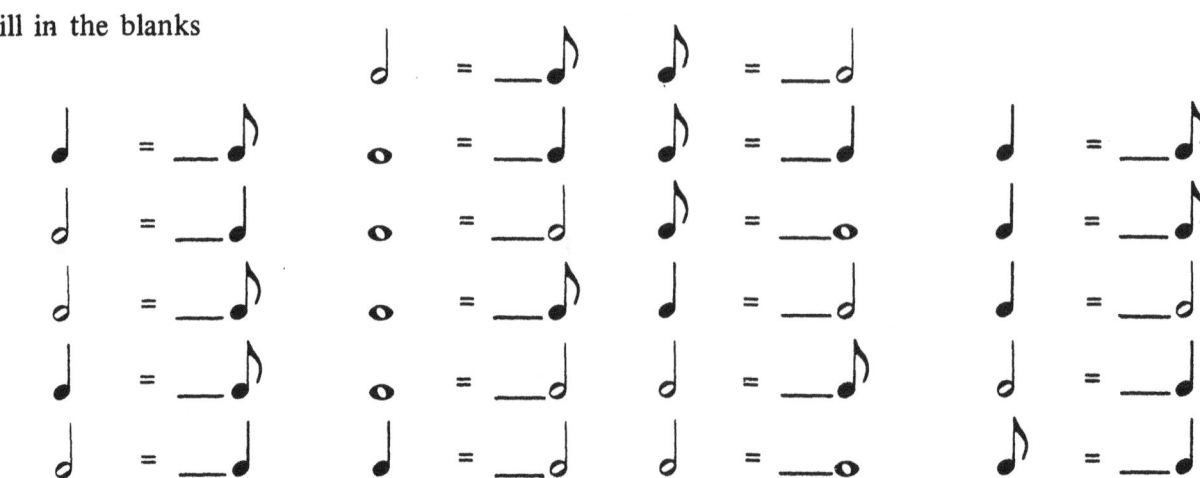

RHYTHM PRACTICE — RESTS —

Fill in the blanks —

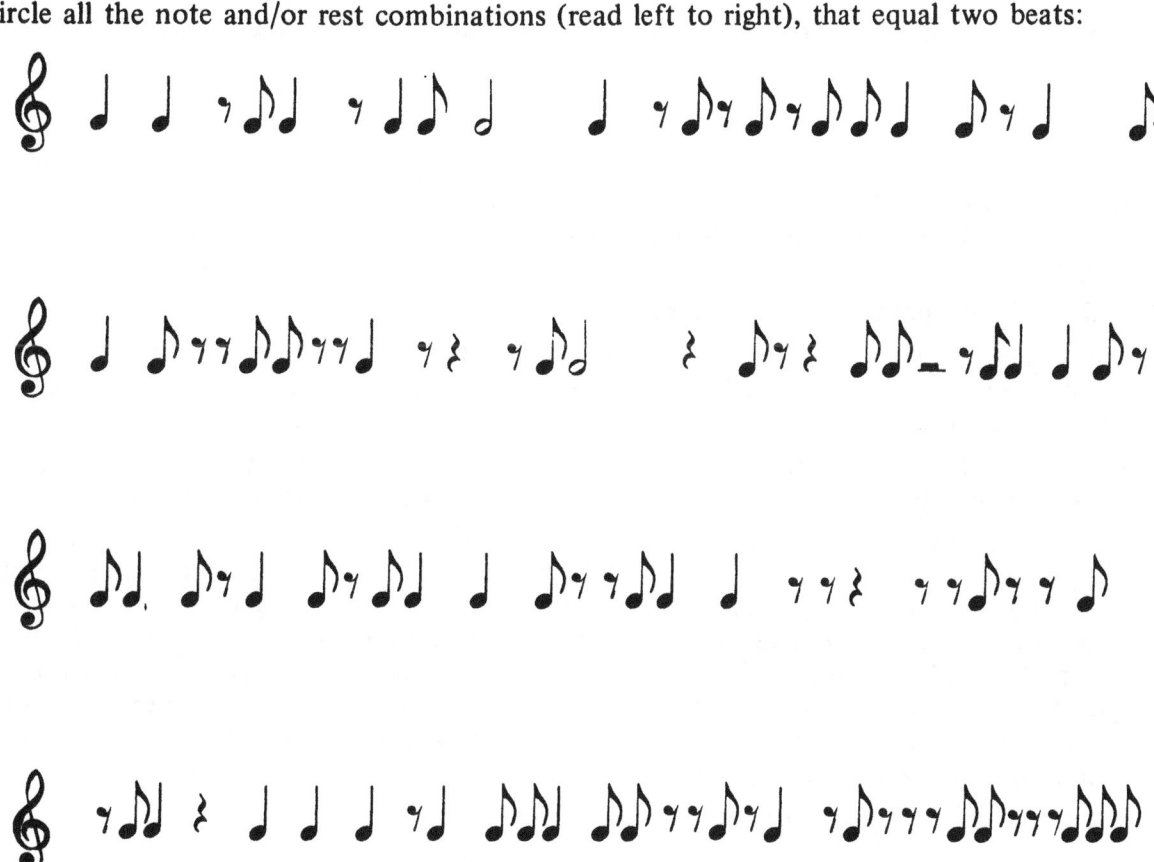

Circle all the note and/or rest combinations (read left to right), that equal two beats:

31

We know that rests are equal to notes in keeping time. How can we practice reading rests and notes? Do we need the guitar?

COUNTING RHYTHM

To avoid the confusion of playing the guitar when you are first learning to read rhythm, you can count the rhythm out loud. This is a professional technique used whenever there is a confusing measure of music. The idea is to assign a different sound to notes and rests. You can use any syllables you like. We will use "dah" for notes and "dee" for rests. It is also quite common to use "dah" for notes, and say nothing for rests. This gives you the sound of the notes and rests as you'll hear them when you play.

To practice counting rhythm, set a tempo by tapping your foot or hand, and then begin to read the rhythm, saying "dah" for each note you see, and   nothing for each rest. It is very important to realize that you must be precise in doing this. You are training your ear — so begin and cut off notes and rests exactly, and hold the notes for their full value.

There is another more involved way to count rhythm that you may prefer. This is the drummer's way. With your left hand you tap out an even pulse, and with your right hand you 'play' the notes (leaving the rests silent). It is complicated at first, but can really be good for your coordination.

DAH DAH DAH DAH   DAH — DAH DAH DAH DAH — DAH DAH DAH   DAH — DAH DAH —

Sight reading rhythm depends upon recognizing notes and rests in PATTERNS. It is impossible to count out every beat as you play, especially at fast tempos. You must recognize the group of notes as a total sound.

We will deal with patterns in two ways.

1. First, each new note or group of notes will be derived — that is, we will see the different components of the note value or pattern, by themselves. We will show how they are arranged to make a pattern, and how it sounds.

2. The second step in learning the pattern is to practice seeing the pattern in among other notes. In fact, recognizing patterns that occur next to each other frequently will soon become easy.

Following are some examples with simple patterns. Count out these examples. As you try to increase your speed, you'll realize the need to keep your eye in front of what you're counting (or playing). Training your eye is something you must practice like your picking. You must go very slowly through an example, and see just how far in front you can look while still playing or counting measures behind. .This is something that comes gradually with regular daily practice. Do not expect overnight magic. You can practice this as you learn more rhythms. Continue on through this section and memorize the new notes and patterns as you will be instructed. But all the while keep using an earlier exercise and practice forcing your eye to the right.

Our first pattern is the eighth note and eighth rest.

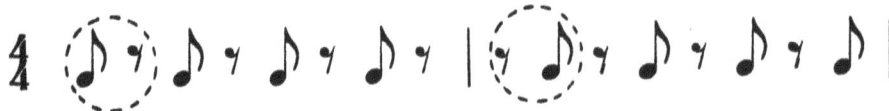

In the following examples, try dividing the measure up into halves (two beats) or even into one beat groups. Think of every eighth note and its accompanying rest (it MUST make up one beat!) as a unit.

32

Practice seeing the patterns in this exercise. After it has become easy, try reading down column 1
and up column 2, down column 3, and so on. Then begin in the bottom right hand corner and start
back . . . . .

41

Continue your reading and eye training with these exercises . . . . .

O.K. Let's put rhythm and pitch together. All of the following exercises are in the key of C major. Play them in the open position, then position 2a, and finally position 4e. WORK SLOWLY AND CAREFULLY. If necessary, count every exercise out loud before playing it.

Remember your steps for new exercises. Count the rhythm, then check the key signature, time signature, and the position you want to use.

Play in position 2a, then 4e,

BEFORE WE CONTINUE . . .

Before we get into more rhythm, we'd like to expose you to more KEYS, the notes in them, and where they appear on the fingerboard. You can practice reading rhythm with any notes, so why not get used to all the notes on the fingerboard instead of just a few. It will be more interesting, and you'll be learning more in less time.

READING AND KEYS . . .

We are going to give a brief introduction to reading in 6 of the 12 keys. We will be using fingerings you know, in new places on the guitar. Remember, a 2a pattern means you begin the scale on the A string with your second finger. But on which note on the A string? The key signature will tell you which note to begin on by what key you are in. If there are no sharps or flats, the key is C, so you put your second finger on the C note on the A string (third fret). That is why it is important to know how many sharps or flats there are in the key signature of each key. (See the appendix on scales.)

When you begin your pattern (which is a major scale . . . all of the patterns you know so far are), you will play all the notes in the scale of C. The KEY of C contains all those notes, so you will be playing where you can find all the notes, if you are playing in a C SCALE position. Sometimes you will see notes that do not belong in the key you are playing in (F# in the key of C for instance). But you can find these notes easily because they are just above or below a note you already know in position by one fret.

When playing in keys like E♭, with several sharps or flats in the key signature, don't worry. If the notes are in the scale, you know where they are by the scale position you are in. In fact, after some practice you will even begin to forget about positions. You will just know where notes are, like walking . . . you don't have to keep an eye on your feet.

For the time being just proceed through the book slowly and carefully. All this information will unfold before you as we go.

CHAPTER 7

Let's take a look at all of the material we've covered so far. You know the names of the notes on the staff and on the ledger lines (up to a point—we'll learn more ledger line notes in chapter 2). You have been introduced to sharps, flats, key signatures, and how to read in the open position and in 2a-C, 2e-G, and 4e-C. In addition you've studied the principles of rhythm and time notation, and you can read and count Eighth notes. When you think of that, it's really quite a bit for 35 pages or so. What's the next step? Let's blow up the myths about how hard it is to read in key   signatures with sharps and flats in them.

Read the following exercises in position 4e key of C. Watch out for the sharps and flats. The fingering is shown to help you find   new notes that may occur.

Well . . . How was it? As you continue playing these exercises you'll find that new notes (like that Bb) are not really <u>that</u> hard to find, IN A POSITION YOU ARE ALREADY FAMILIAR WITH. Let's look at some new scale fingerings that can make reading some of these new notes even easier.

POSITION 4a

This position takes us into a new key, with new notes. The new key is F major. It has all the notes of the key of C, except that the B is now lowered to Bb.

This position begins on the A string with your fourth finger.

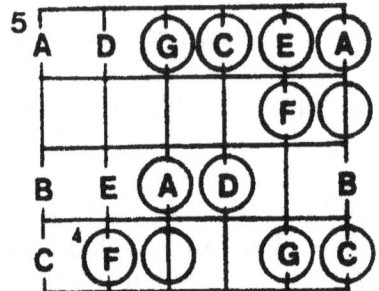

Advantages:
Scale is very easy to finger. Position of scale is close to C scale 4e, Bb scale 2e, and enables you to play in higher parts of F scale without long stretches

This position also moves well to reach keys like Eb and Db in their lower parts.

Let's try some reading in this new position. The only difference between 4a F and 4e C is that the 4a F scale contains a Bb note instead of a B note. ALL OF THE OTHER NOTES ARE THE SAME FOR BOTH SCALES.

F major scale   F G A Bb C D E F
C major scale   C D E F G A B C
F major scale   C D E F G A Bb C
(rearranged)

Compare the fingerings below and then play the following exercises in 4a F.

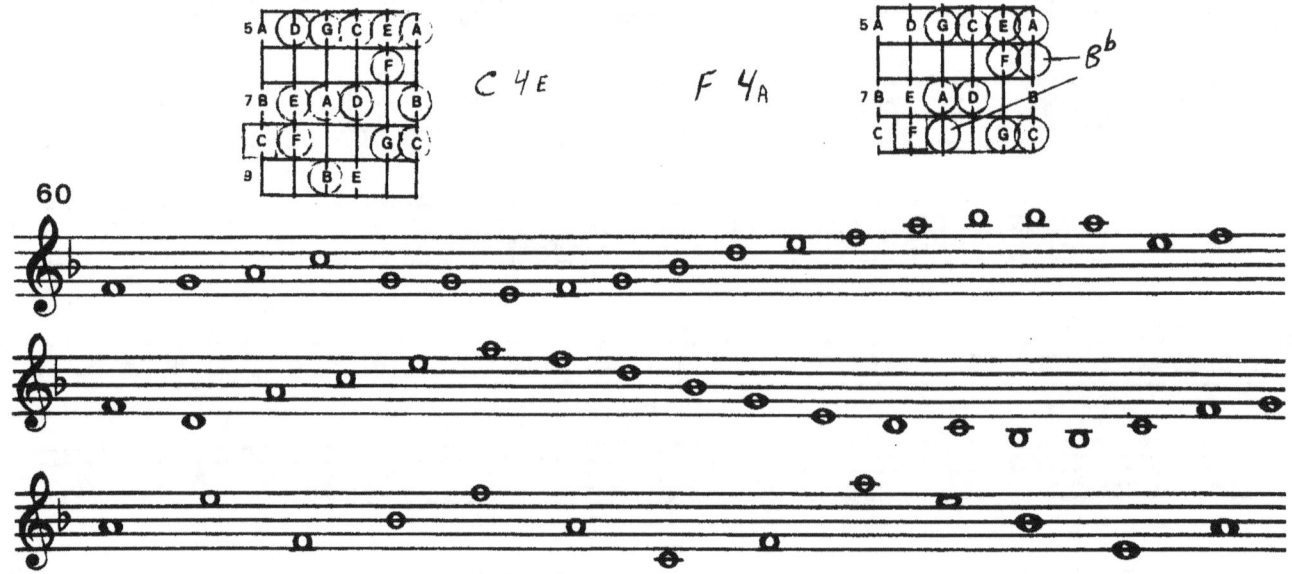

60

38

61

62

63

64

Let's continue this idea one step farther. There are other notes we have not played in the 4e C position. What about playing some of the Eb notes? Find these Eb notes on your guitar as they're shown in the diagram below and then try the following exercises.

65

The key of Bb major has both the Bb note in it, and the Eb note in it. We could use a Bb major scale fingering to learn where these notes are, in the same way   we used a C major scale fingering to learn where the seven natural notes were.   (the notes that are contained in the C major scale.)

Bb major scale Bb C D Eb F G A B♭
C major scale C D E F G A B C
Bb major scale C D <u>Eb</u> F G A <u>Bb</u> C
(rearranged)

Now compare the 2e fingering of a Bb MAJOR SCALE (not G. . .) With the 4e C major scale, as shown in the diagrams below.

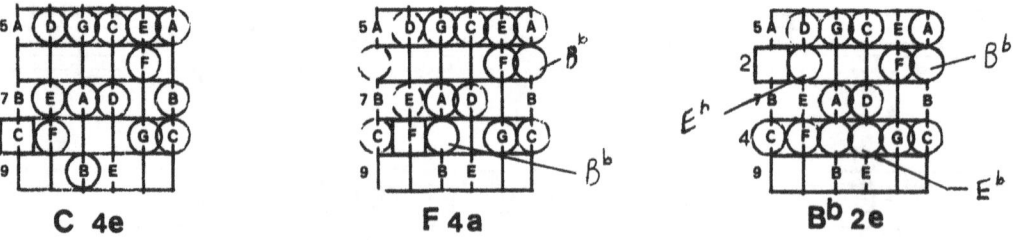

Can you see all the notes that are the same in all three of these scales?

When you read in 4 a F you had to keep your mind on the new note—the Bb. Gradually you became more familiar with it. Soon (if not already) it will be as easy to read as in the good ol' key of C, 4e. Now we've given you another new note to deal with, the Eb note. We're going to do the same thing as before. Gradually you'll become familiar with the location of the Eb note IN RELATION TO WHAT YOU ALREADY KNOW. Play the following exercises in 2e-Bb. Before you play each exercise, play the scale fingering several times so you can keep remembering where those Eb notes are found.

40

Well we have really been playing a lot up in that area around 4e-C. Let's look to other areas of the fingerboard and see what other keys we can become familiar with.

If you recall, we have previously learned to read down here in the key of C major (using that 2a fingering) and in the key of G major (using the 2e fingering). There was only one note difference between the two keys. The G scale had an F#, while the C scale had an F (to be comfortable from here on I suggest you go back and play pages 21/2 where we first used these fingerings in this position). At first the F# note was a new note and therefore a problem. But the more you played it the easier it got to be. We're going to continue the process of finding new notes in this position as we did in the 4e C position. We'll add one new note at a time and relate it to a MAJOR SCALE FINGERING.

You are already familiar with the 4a fingering in the key of F major (down on the 8th fret). Let's move that fingering down to the key of D major, on the Fifth Fret as shown below. Play that scale fingering and then compare it to the G major 2e and C major 2a fingerings shown to the right.

C major scale C D E F G A B C
G major scale G A B C D E F# G
D major scale D E F# G A B C# D

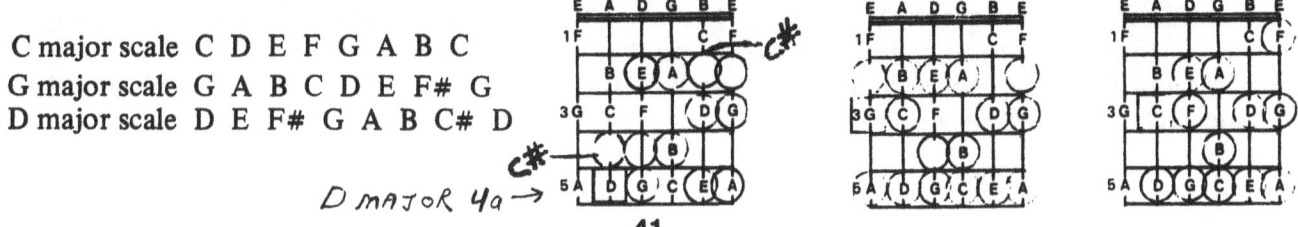

41

70a

b

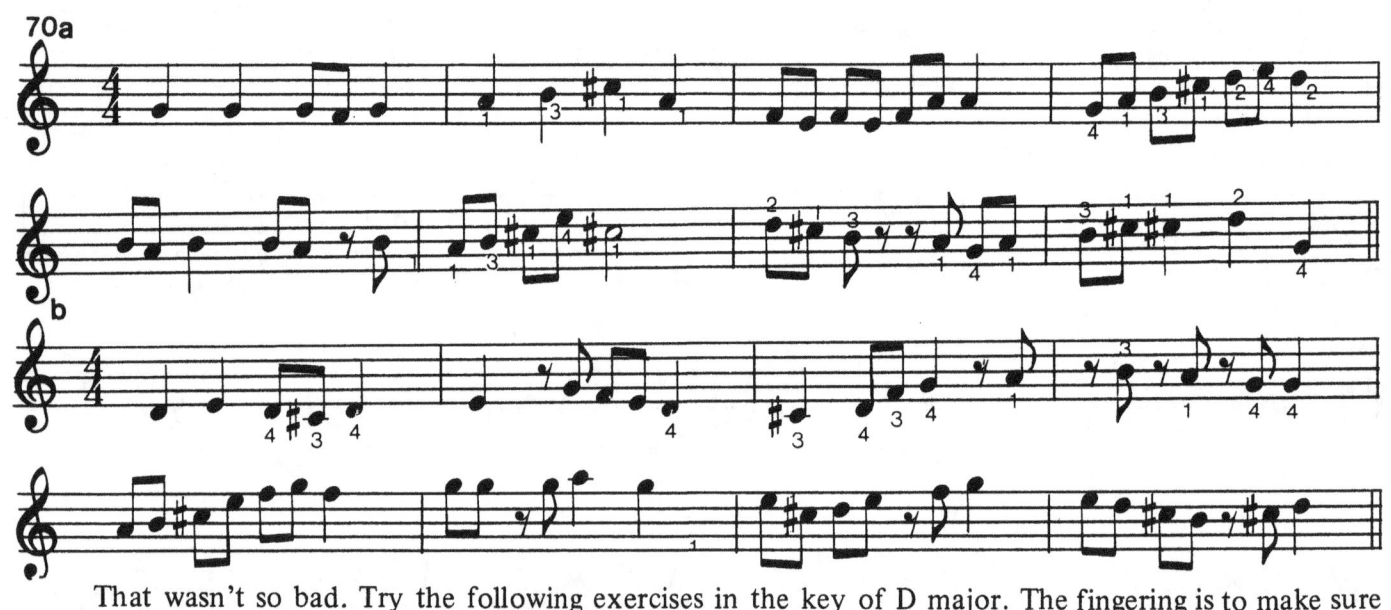

That wasn't so bad. Try the following exercises in the key of D major. The fingering is to make sure you play the right notes as you first begin here. . .

71 a

b

72 a

b

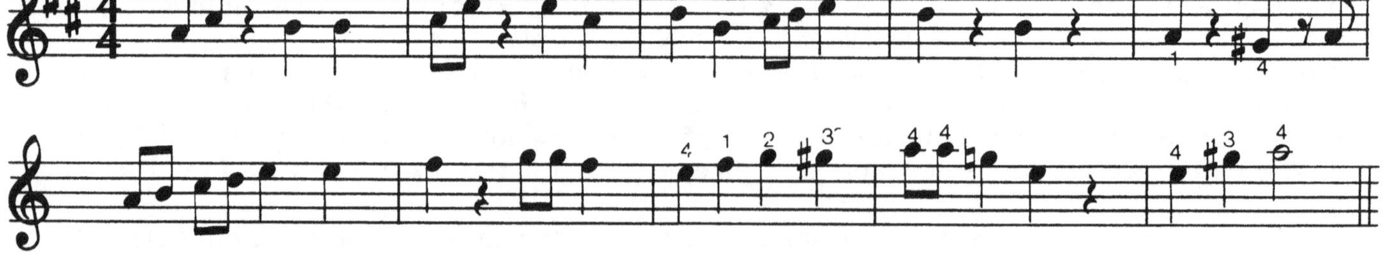

We can carry this strategy forward one more step to the key of A major. The A major scale introduces another new note beyond the notes we have already seen, the G# note. We are still in the same location . . . 2e G, we're just adding notes we haven't seen yet. Compare the three scales below and locate the new G# note. We're using an old friend, the 4e fingering, except we're playing it from the root A instead of C, where you first saw it.

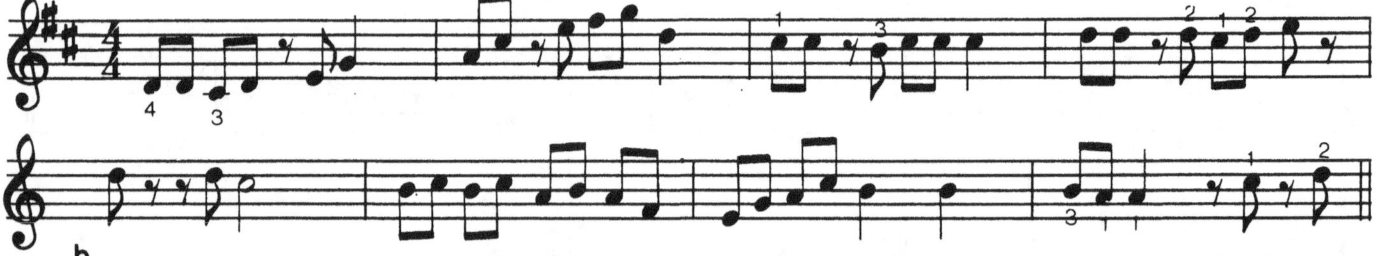

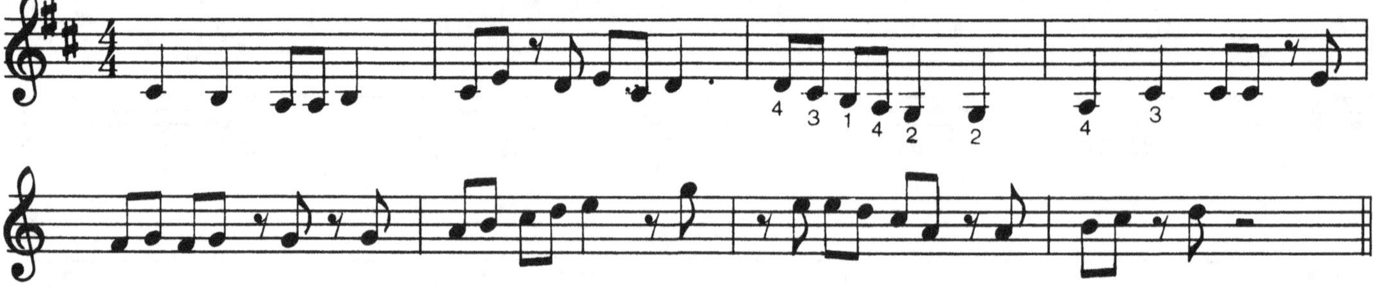

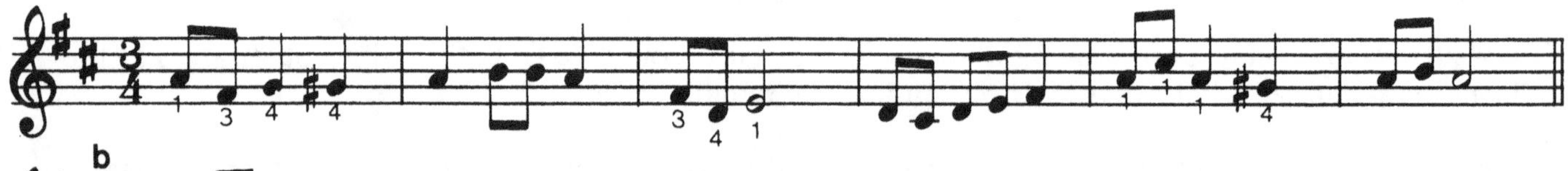

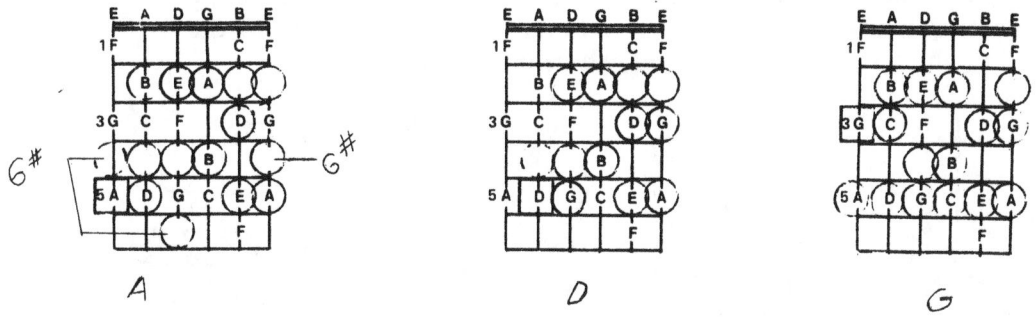

Try the following exercises in your new A 4e fingering, this time for the key of A major.

73 a

b

74 a

b

75 a

b

76 a

b

If you're having trouble here, go more slowly and review this entire chapter. This is a step by step process that can open up the entire fingerboard to you, if you do every step. . .

Our overall strategy for learning new keys and positions: The keys lock together into groups because of the way the scale fingerings lock together. The first group you saw was in the 4e C area. 4e C, 4a F, 2e Bb and 2a Eb (which we haven't done yet) all belong in this group.

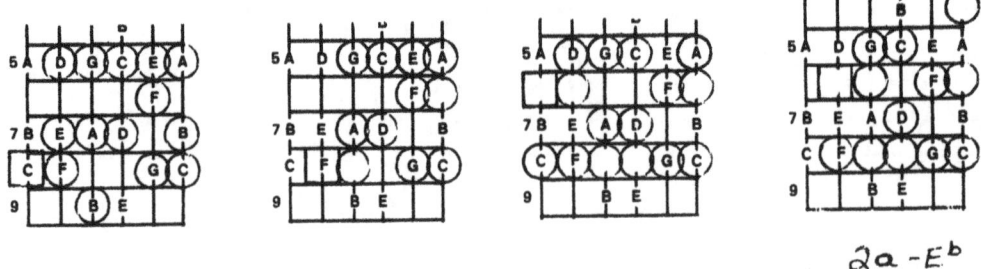

The second group we just finished had 2a C, 2e G, 4a D, and 4e A in it.

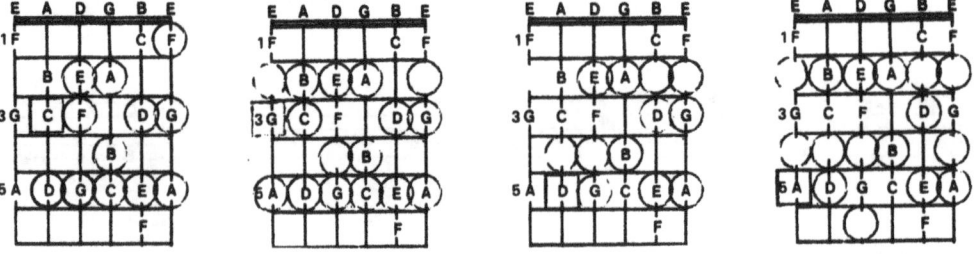

The next group will begin in a brand new location—2e key of A. Here we'll have 2e A, 2a D, 4a E and 4e B.

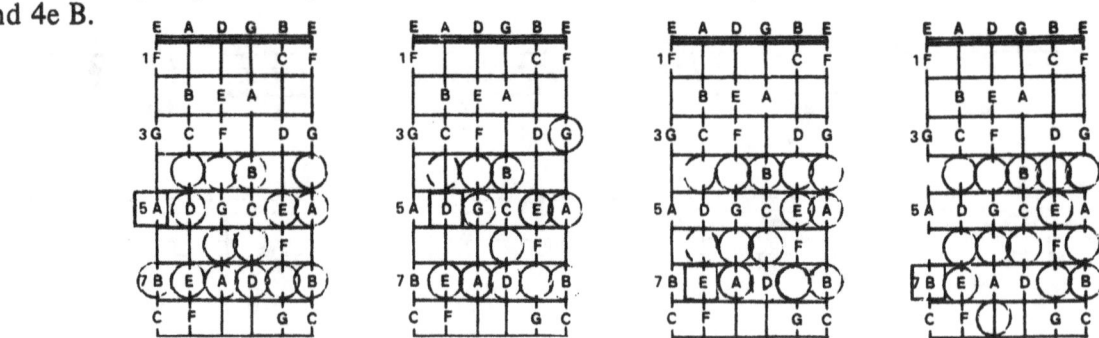

The next group would also be new. You could start with an easy Bb scale—4e. From that location you could read in Eb 4a, Ab 2e, and into the dreaded key of Db in 2a.

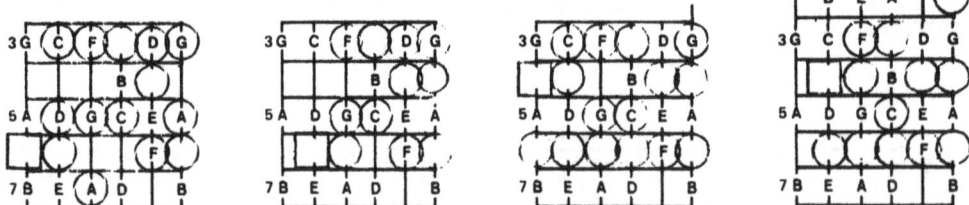

There are other groups you could do also. What about starting in 4e D major. That would give you 4a G major. 2e C major, and 2a F major   Because of the size of this book and the number of pages of exercises required to go through the different keys, we will be unable to do them all.
You should be reading as much outside material as possible using the strategy of positions described above.

Before continuing with our study of Rhythm, there are some other scale fingerings that are available for reading. Memorize each fingering and then try it in a few exercises. Give each of these fingerings a fair chance. They are good for reading AND they are very useful for improvising. (You'll find these major scale fingerings used in Leon's book on improvising STYLES FOR THE STUDIO—the publisher.)

POSITION 1e

This position is for a G scale; the only sharp in the scale, and the key, is F#. The fingering is shown on the diagram. The scale is named 1e because you are starting on the E string with your first finger.

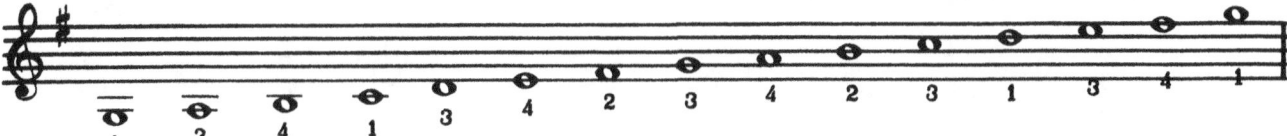

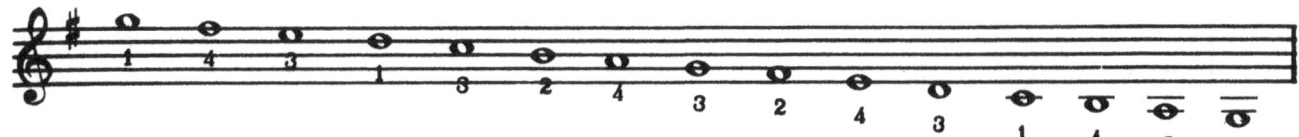

Advantages:
You are able to reach high B without shifting your hand. Also — you NEVER have to leave this position to reach notes that aren't in the scale in this range. That is, all the Ab, Bb, Db, and Eb notes between the low G and high B fall under your fingers.

Disadvantages:
It is inconvenient to reach the low F# with your first finger already on low G.

POSITION 1a

This position is for the C major scale. It begins on the fifth string with your first finger.

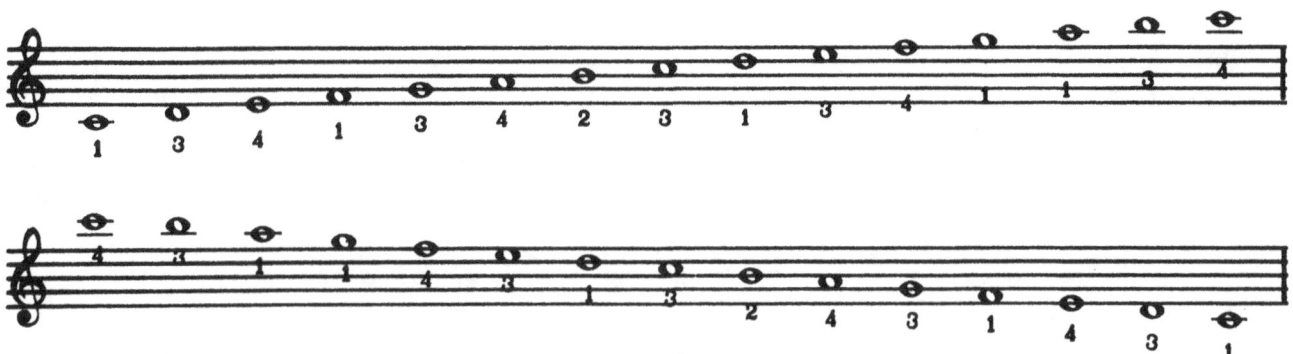

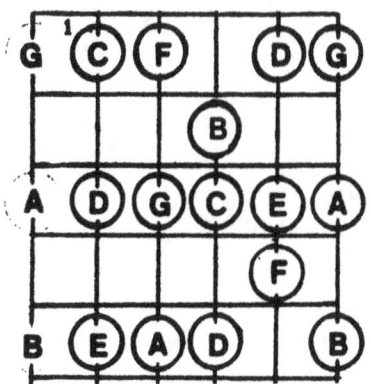

Advantages:
Like the scale position 1e, this position also makes playing non-scale notes like Ab, Bb, Db, Eb, and Gb easy because you don't have to leave position.

Disadvantages:
There is a shift required to reach upper scale tones. (A, B, and C). And of course, like 1e, the low F also requires a shift.

Play all your exercises to here in this position. This is important.

FIGURES . . .

If you recall, we have discussed the fact that notes and rests will fall into patterns that we will frequently see. These patterns should be memorized so that they can be quickly recognized as you read. You have seen a 1 beat figure with the eighth note and eighth rest.

Now we are going to give you some easy 2 beat figures . . . . .

AND

CHAPTER 8

EXTENDED NOTES . . .

There are two very common devices used to increase the length of time you hold a note.

1. **The tie** — A tie is a curved line connecting two notes OF THE SAME PITCH. When you see a tie, you play the first note only, and hold the sound for the length of both notes.

2. **The dot** — The dot is a device used to increase any note by half its own value. That is, a quarter note is equal to two eighth notes. But a quarter note with a dot after it is equal to three eighth notes.

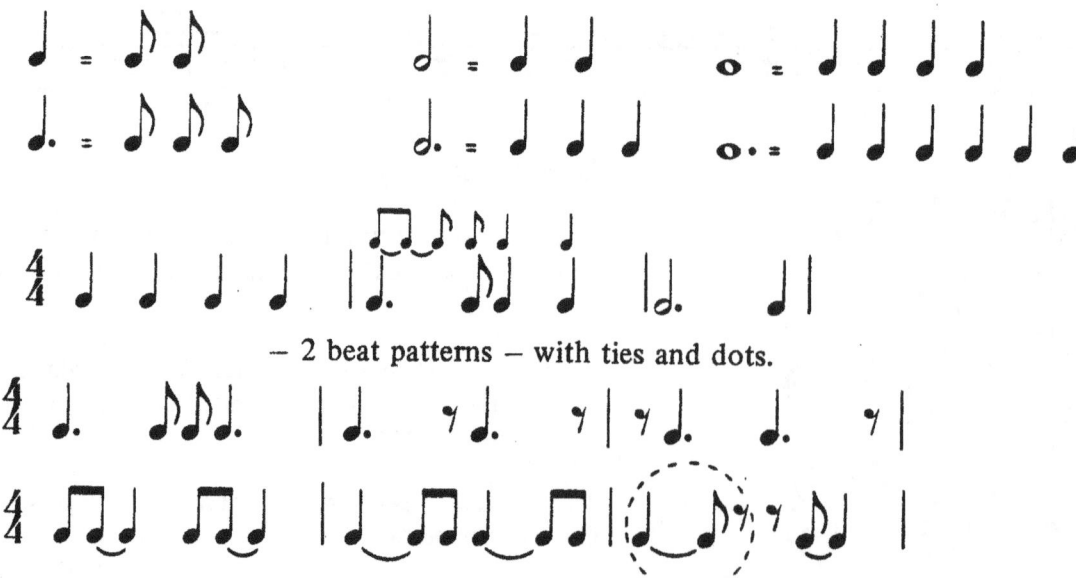

— 2 beat patterns — with ties and dots.

Following are some exercises with ties and dots. Watch for patterns. If you get confused with ties, count the measure without them FIRST, then add them.

87

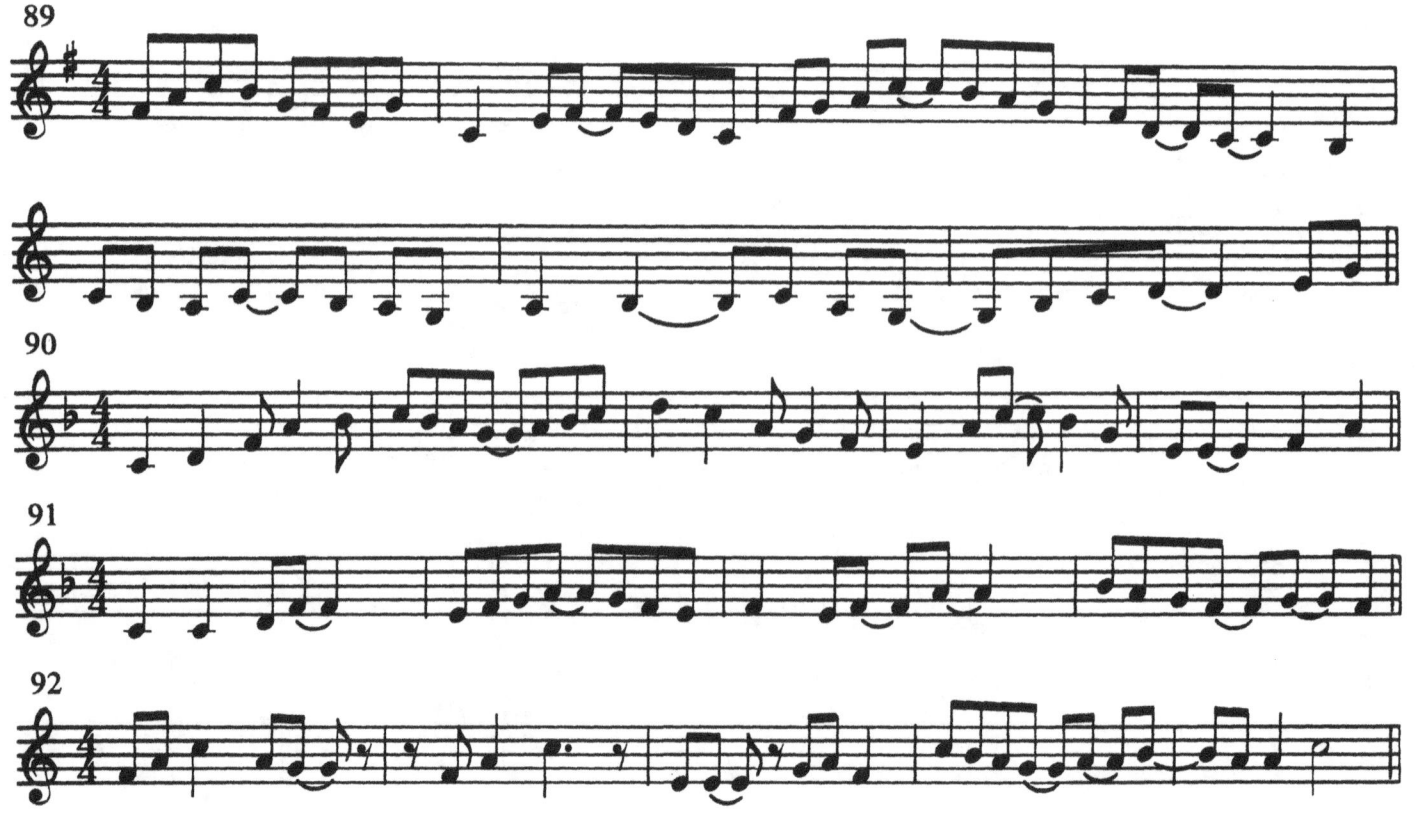

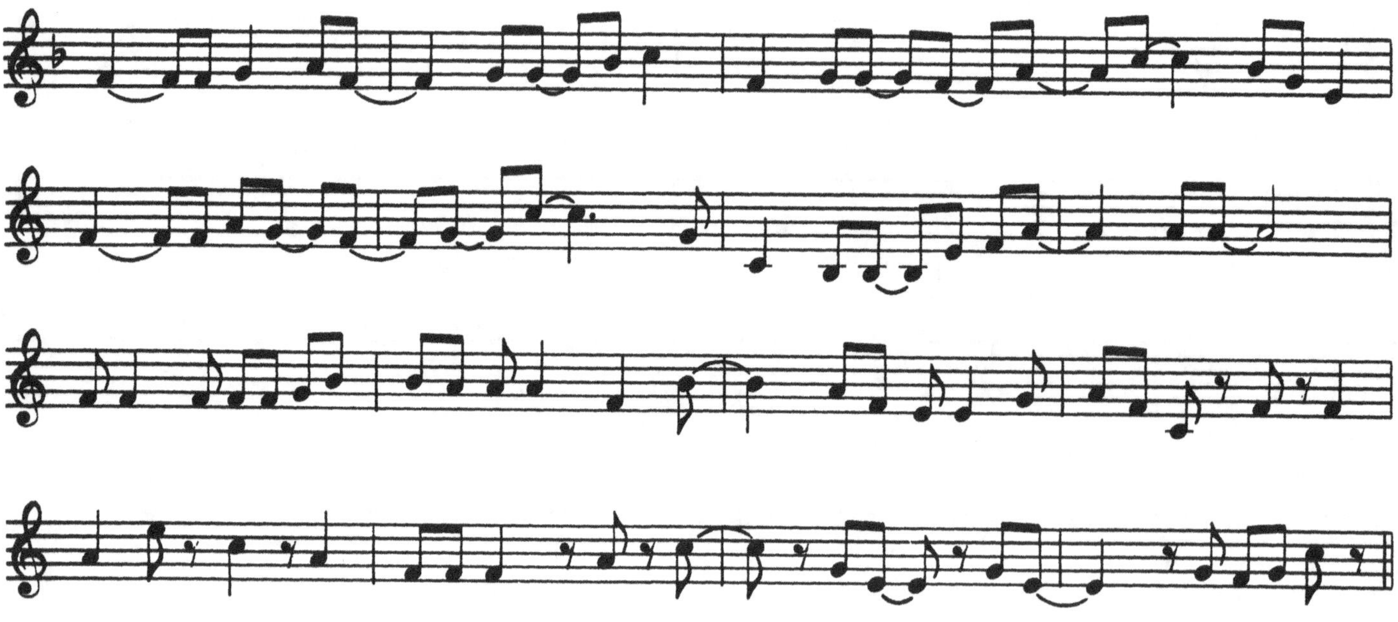

88

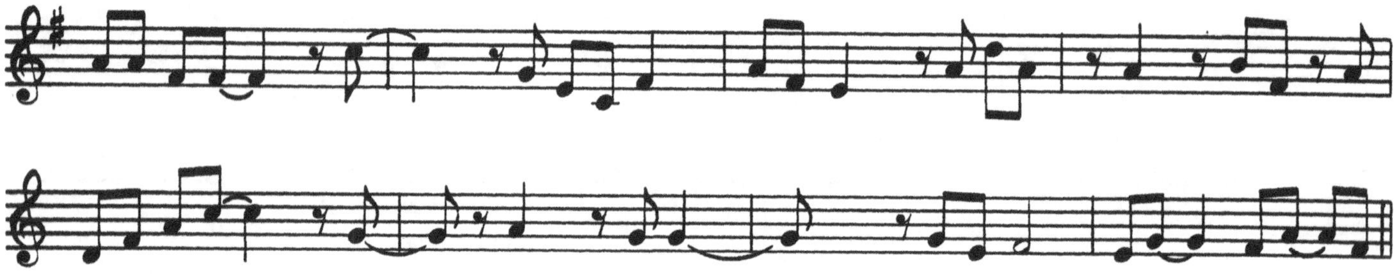

TIES! TIES!! Watch out for figures. You can even circle them in pencil if it helps.

89

90

91

92

MORE TIES!

49

CHAPTER 9

This is a new note — It's called the "sixteenth" note.
It is 1/4 of a quarter note.   1/4 x 1/4 = 1/16.   It's 1/2 of an eighth note.
Both the rest and the note have two flags.

Watch out! In the time you used to play one eighth note, you now have to play two sixteenth notes. Slow down your tempos if you have trouble at the start.

Before, we divided one beat up to have TWO PULSES in it. With sixteenth notes we can now have FOUR PULSES PER BEAT. If it helps to learn this, think of each beat as a miniature BAR of $\frac{4}{4}$.

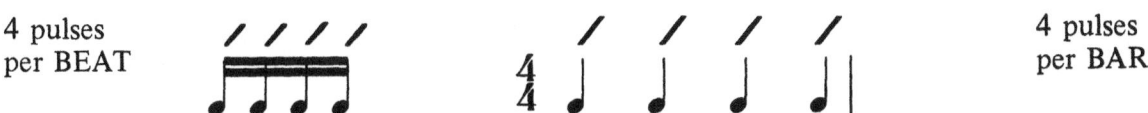

4 pulses per BEAT   4 pulses per BAR

Each one has four pulses in it, with a note played on each pulse, but your familiarity with quarter notes in $\frac{4}{4}$ may help you to hear the sound more easily. To change from thinking in the 'miniature bar' to the single beat, count the miniature bar and tap your foot only on the first note – repeat this, speeding up the tempo until you're playing four notes per beat – that is what the four sixteenths sound like. We will use this 'miniature bar' idea throughout the rest of the book, in explaining more complicated beats.

For now, remember that with these four SIXTEENTHS you are playing TWO on the down tap of your foot, and TWO on the up swing of each SINGLE BEAT.

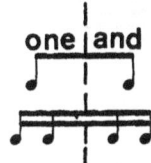

one | and

Count the examples below, then play, in your 2a position.

100

101

One beat figures using the sixteenth note — The examples on the left show how the whole beat is broken up into sixteenth notes. On the right is the common notation for each of the sounds. Remember that you play the first note of a tie and hold the sound for the total length of both notes.

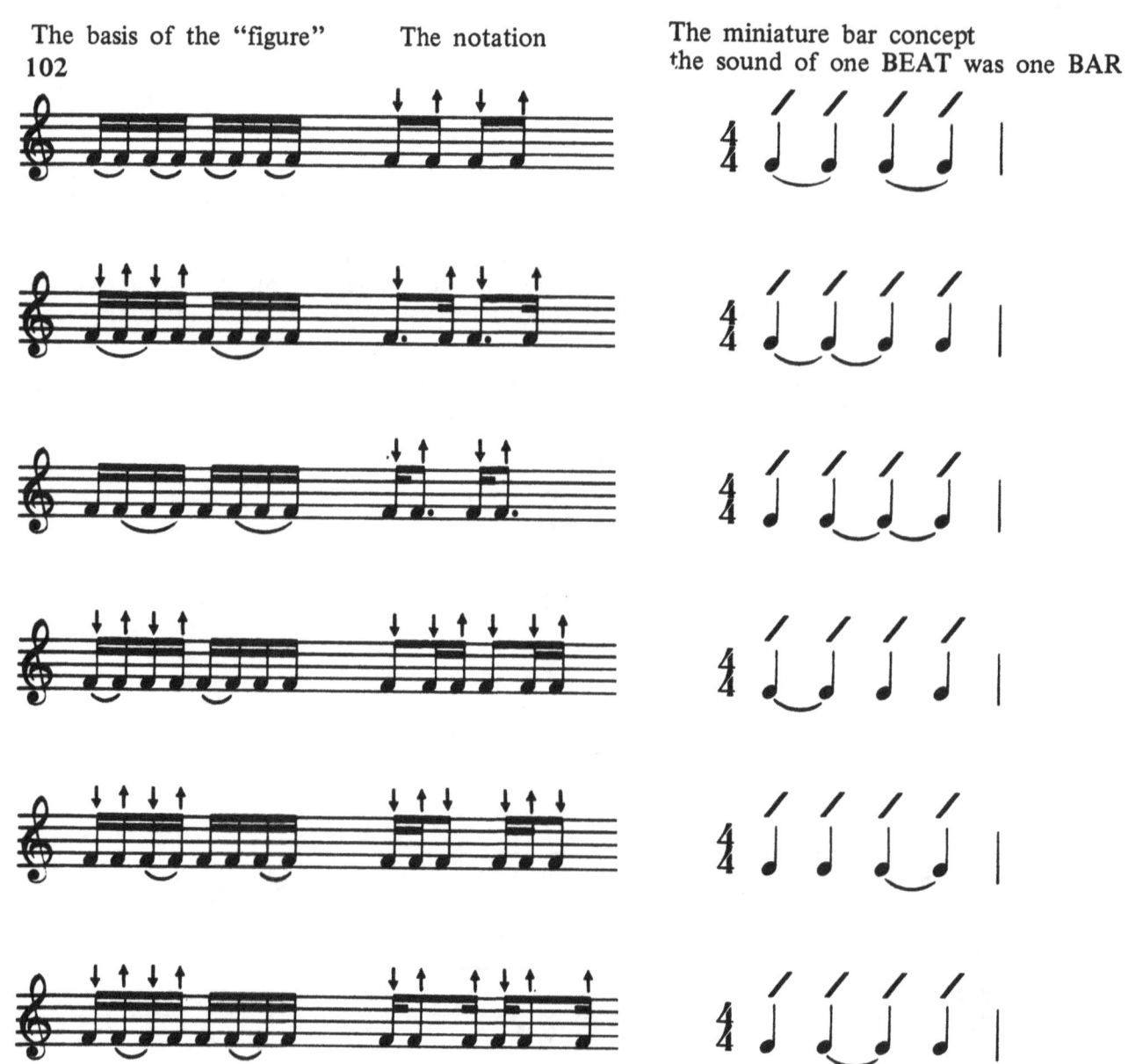

MEMORIZE ALL
OF THESE SOUNDS,
AND THE "FIGURE"
THAT GOES WITH
IT.

YOU MUST KNOW
THESE!!

To keep the time clear, visualize each beat as two parts: two eighth notes (or the corresponding sixteenths). OBSERVE PICKING!!!

Count the following exercises twice before playing. Play slowly! PRACTICE the correct picking till you can feel the 'up' half of each beat.

103

104

105

106

107

108

109

110

111 Count this exercise very slowly.

116

117

118

119

Take your time here. Once you recognize the sound of each figure with its tie, try to remember it —
Try to think of these as TWO beat 'figures.'

120

121

122

Now let's add some melody to all this rhythm.

CHAPTER 10

THE TRIPLET

Say "one-trip-let" — that is the sound of a triplet. All three pulses are played in one beat.

We have divided the beat into halves and quarters — now let's divide it into three EQUAL parts.
The resulting figure is called a triplet, and is played like it is counted. "ONE TRIPLET"

TRIPLET: Three notes played in the time of TWO NOTES OF THE SAME VALUE.

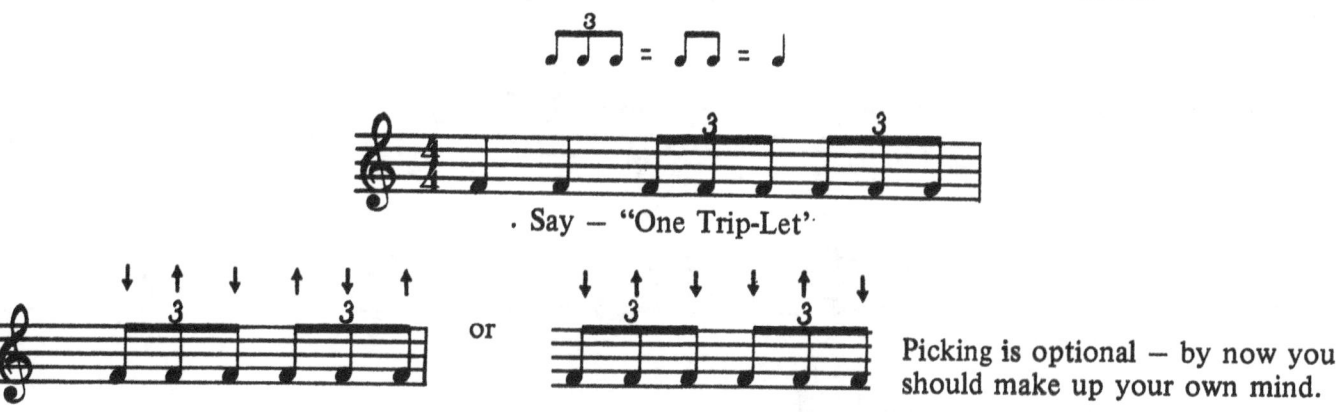

. Say — "One Trip-Let"

or

Picking is optional — by now you
should make up your own mind.

Remember, count these exercises first before playing them. Then play slowly.

144

145

146

147

148

149 Count these exercises slowly first – then play slowly

62

Triplets may be tied together . . .

Count these slowly to get the sound — then MEMORIZE THE SOUND OF EACH.

THE BASIS OF THE FIGURE **THE NOTATION**

154 Play these exercises very slowly. Don't leave this page until you know them all!

Triplets may also be subdivided.

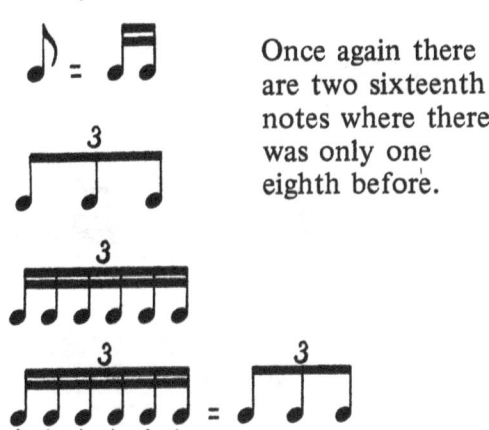

Once again there are two sixteenth notes where there was only one eighth before.

MEMORIZE THE SOUND OF THESE THREE

Picking here is of your own option. I suggest that you just alternate (↓ ↑).

168

174

175

176

CHAPTER 11

Here are more triplet subdivisions

A triplet is three notes in the time of two of the same value.

Watch your picking!!! BE CONSISTENT in whatever way you play each figure.

The last of the triplet subdivisions! (Part 1)

On the right are bars of $\frac{3}{4}$ that may help you hear the triplets more easily . . . they sound the same*

*That is — in a triplet you are dividing a beat into three pulses — in a bar of $\frac{3}{4}$ you have three pulses — so a bar of three four is 'equivalent' to one triplet beat. Count the bar of three four and then speed it up by feeling it in one. Count 1 2 3 1 2 3 at first. Then just try it by feeling 1 . .   1 . . It may help you to keep track of the picking. These figures you should memorize.

184

Triplet subdivision — part 2

Count all of these slowly!!

CHAPTER 12

LEDGER LINES — BASS CLEF

We are now going to enter new territory; new places to read notes, and new places to play notes. There are two areas of study in this part. There are higher notes than we have seen (ledger lines) and there are lower notes written in a different way (the bass clef). The notes in the bass clef are the same low notes we have seen before, but they are written differently. There will be occasions when you will need to read in this clef, so it is important to explore.

The notes on the lines are A C E and G.

Speak the name of the notes out loud, if it helps.

BASS CLEF

For ease of printing and comprehension, it has been standard to notate guitar pitches one octave higher than they sound. If we didn't do this, you would have to read on two staves, like piano, or on five ledger lines most of the time. While this has not affected your playing, it is important to know, especially when tuning to other instruments.

Written for guitar
sounds in real pitch

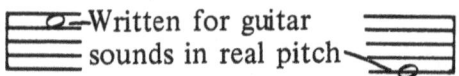

There are occasions when the guitarist must read off of the piano or bass part. So it is important to read bass clef. The pitches will be shown and exercises given in this new clef in relation to the true pitch of the guitar – that is, showing where the pitch really sounds.

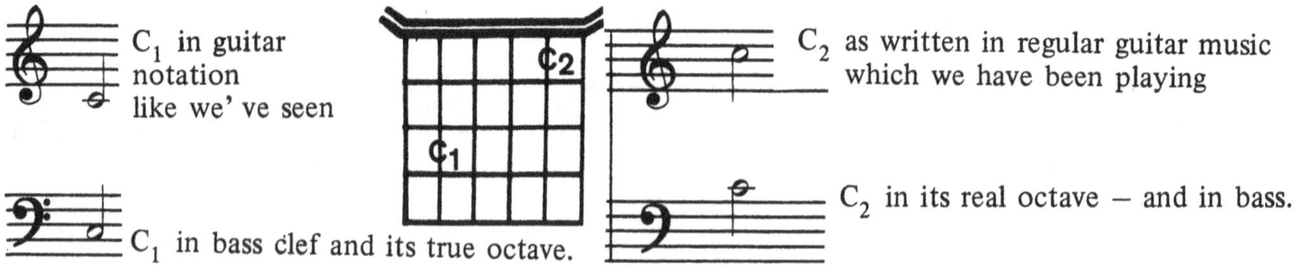

C1 in guitar notation like we' ve seen
C2
C1
C2 as written in regular guitar music which we have been playing
C1 in bass clef and its true octave.
C2 in its real octave – and in bass.

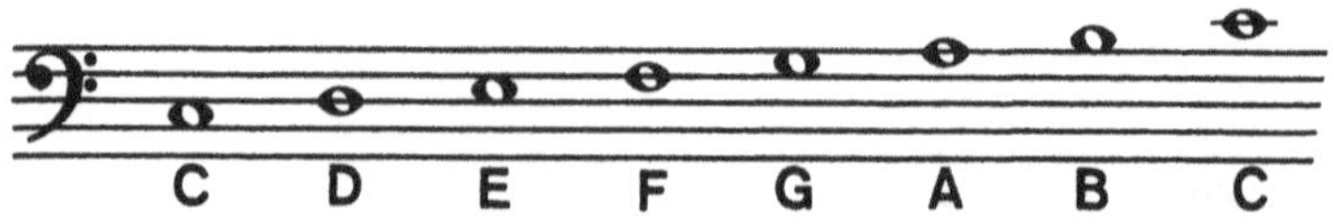

C D E F G A B C

Use scale position 2a

E A D G B E
F C F
B E A
G C F D G
B
A D G C E A

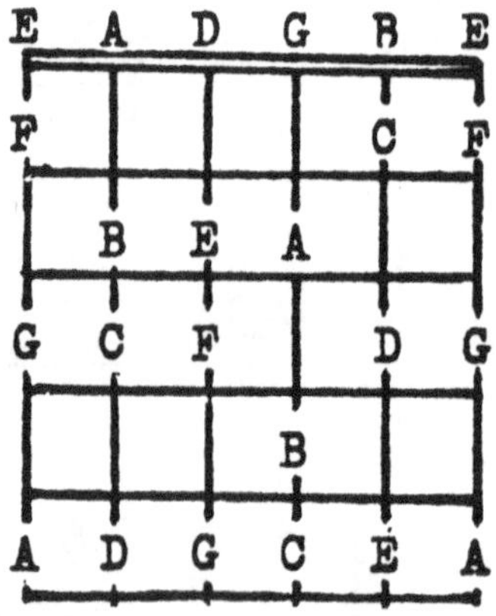

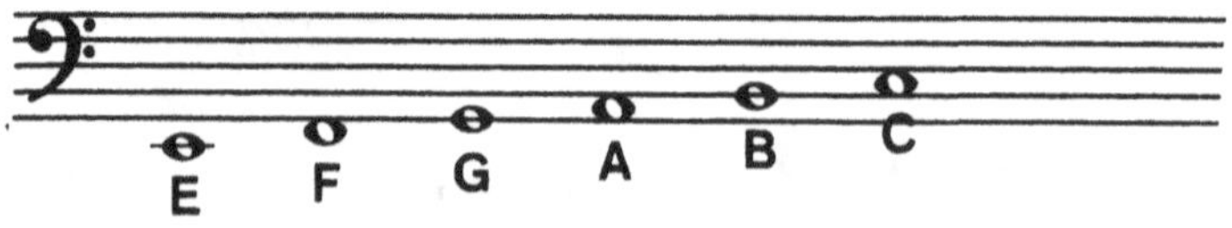

E F G A B C

Use 2a scale position here also

Fingers 0 1 2 4 1 2

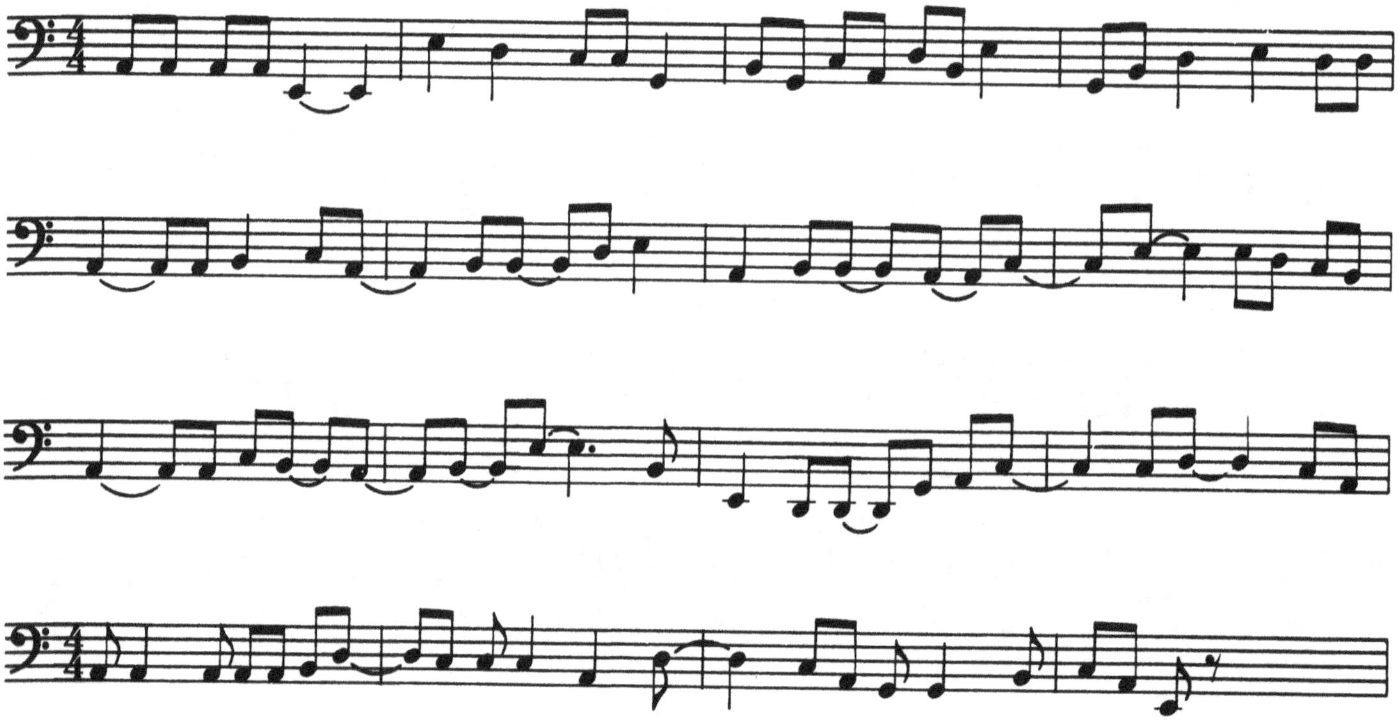

CHAPTER 13 — READING CHORDS . . . .

This book has been using only single line note reading to demonstrate the basics of rhythm and pitch. However, if you continue, you will at some point be faced with reading chords.

Why?

You would want to know about chord reading because: 1) you want to be a "super reader" for professional/studio level playing, or 2) you want to be able to figure out someone else's arrangement for guitar so that you can play it from memory. In No. 1 above you must read quickly AT SIGHT!! No. 2 requires only that you be able to figure it out somehow in order to memorize it. You will be at level No. 2 before you can reach No. 1.

How do you get to the level where you can figure out chord spelling and fingerings? Mostly it comes from trying it over and over. You see a chord spelling on paper. What is your first step?

1. Remember what key it is in.

2. Check the highest note, and the lowest of the chord — is there some place where the two are near each other on the guitar neck?

3. Good, you found it. (It has to be there or it can't be played, right?)

4. Now locate the notes one at a time, working from high to low.

5. To remember the chord in the song, try thinking of your hand shape while looking at the chord on the page.

Below are some examples. Try them out;

This exercise is played only on the first four strings. It could be played with a pick or with fingers.

Even here with these extra top voice notes, you could use pick or fingers.

Once you are at level two you can attempt studio type assignments if you are fast at figuring things out. How? What will basically come out on the recording is the top note of the chord, and the basic color. So look at the top note and work down. If you have the alphabet writing to help you (most times it's there), then it's a question of deduction. For example: You see the top note of the jumble is a B. The alphabet says G_7. What Inversion of G_7 do you know with a B note as the top note? Grab that and worry about the other notes later.

What about when you see pure alphabet situation with G_{13-9}? If you can't grab all those color notes at once, get what you can get: G_9 or just G_7. The secret is to stay out of everybody's way until you can get your bearings. If you are faced with a pure block chord reading situation, with no alphabet to help you, and you aren't at that level one where you can zip through it, try adding the alphabet yourself. Look at the chords and figure out what they spell, then play that chord in any inversion you know (or with whatever top note is called for if you can). All block chord is not seen frequently, and when it is, it's usually a special arrangement — so if it looks imposing, you're better off telling the arranger you can't cut it, than to take hours proving it.

What can you expect to see written? Will you always see just one kind of notation?

THE ALPHABET SYSTEM

This system gives you the name of the chord, and when to play it. The slash marks and notes underneath the chord denote only the RHYTHM. They are not related to PITCH. So to master this level of reading you must be able to find chords without looking at your guitar while reading rhythm. That is all.

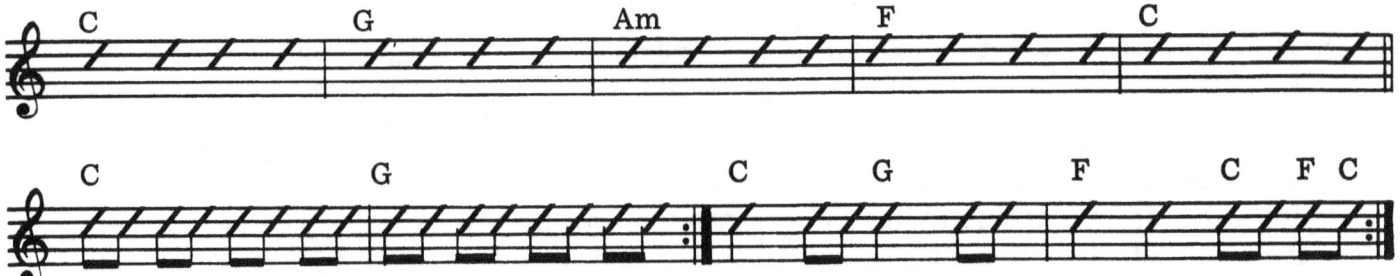

THE ALPHABET AND LINE SYSTEM

This level is like No. 1 except that now the arranger wants to hear the chord with a particular note on top, which he writes. This requires all the knowledge of level one, and more knowledge of chords — enough to know which chord has what note on top (not as hard as it sounds).

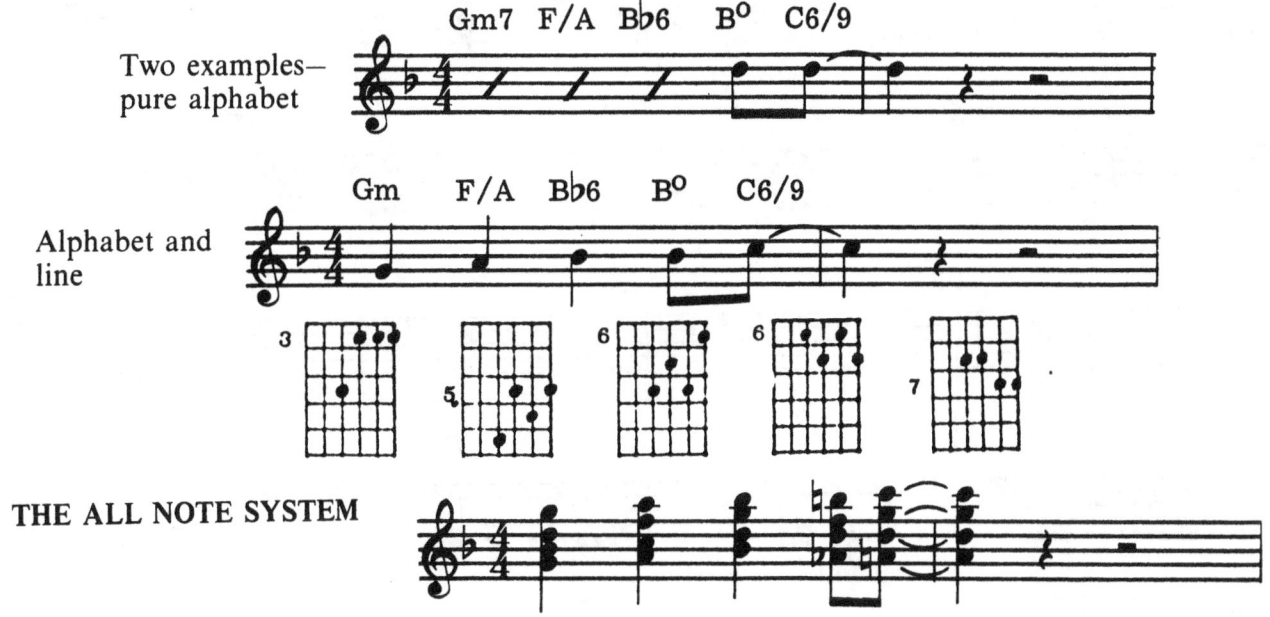

This is the hardest. Here you have to be able to play the chord as written, without looking at your guitar ideally (although there's lots of faking). This level also includes Guitar Arrangements, which usually have moving voices and much more activity overall. Rarely will you ever be asked to read a solo guitar arrangement. However, a block chord arrangement like a movie theme or jingle, is seen, and is read.

So . . . someone arranges a favorite tune of yours for solo guitar. You want to learn it so you get the arrangement. What next?

1. Do you know the melody of the song? It helps to have heard it. Of course this isn't always possible but it does help.

2. Look over the whole song. Does it have repeats? What key is it in? Are there many high passages? What is the tempo?

3. Get a pencil!!!!! The pros always use one to mark whatever they need to help them play.

4. Begin to learn the song by figuring out each chord, one at a time from the top note down (on the staff). Learn a few bars at a time, and commit them to memory.

5. Remember, the music wasn't written as a "stump the guitarist" test. The composer/arranger wants the song to be PLAYED! Don't Panic.

6. The arrangement may be written in several different styles, that require different right hand techniques. Example No. 1 page 79 could be played with a flat pick (or fingers) AS shown, but not if it had moving lines inside the chords. The composer and the kind of song you're reading will tell you a lot. Chet Atkins country arrangements would be very difficult if you didn't play finger style. Conversely, a rock chord figure would only sound right with a flat pick.

7. It is important to note that solo guitar arrangements are most often of a style played with the fingers of the right hand. This is because there is a melody, chord accompaniment, and a bass line all in the arrangement, and all in separate movement at one time or another.

8. There is not a lot of modern music arranged for the guitar yet (although every day more and more music is being written). So you may be faced with trying to get a song from a piano arrangement. To compress it, just think of the melody, the chords under it, and the bass line that moves the chords along. Ted Greene's book, CHORD CHEMISTRY*, contains much information about the movement of chords and bass lines in relation to the melody, when playing solo guitar.

9. Most of all . . . GO SLOWLY, USE YOUR COMMON SENSE, AND DON'T GIVE UP. Chord reading is very advanced guitar playing, but those who can do it (and more and more can) have achieved the highest level of PRO-ficiency in this area. You will know your guitar better than you ever thought possible, and, you will be playing music you never thought you'd even understand!!!! Good luck!   *Also available from D.Z. Publications.

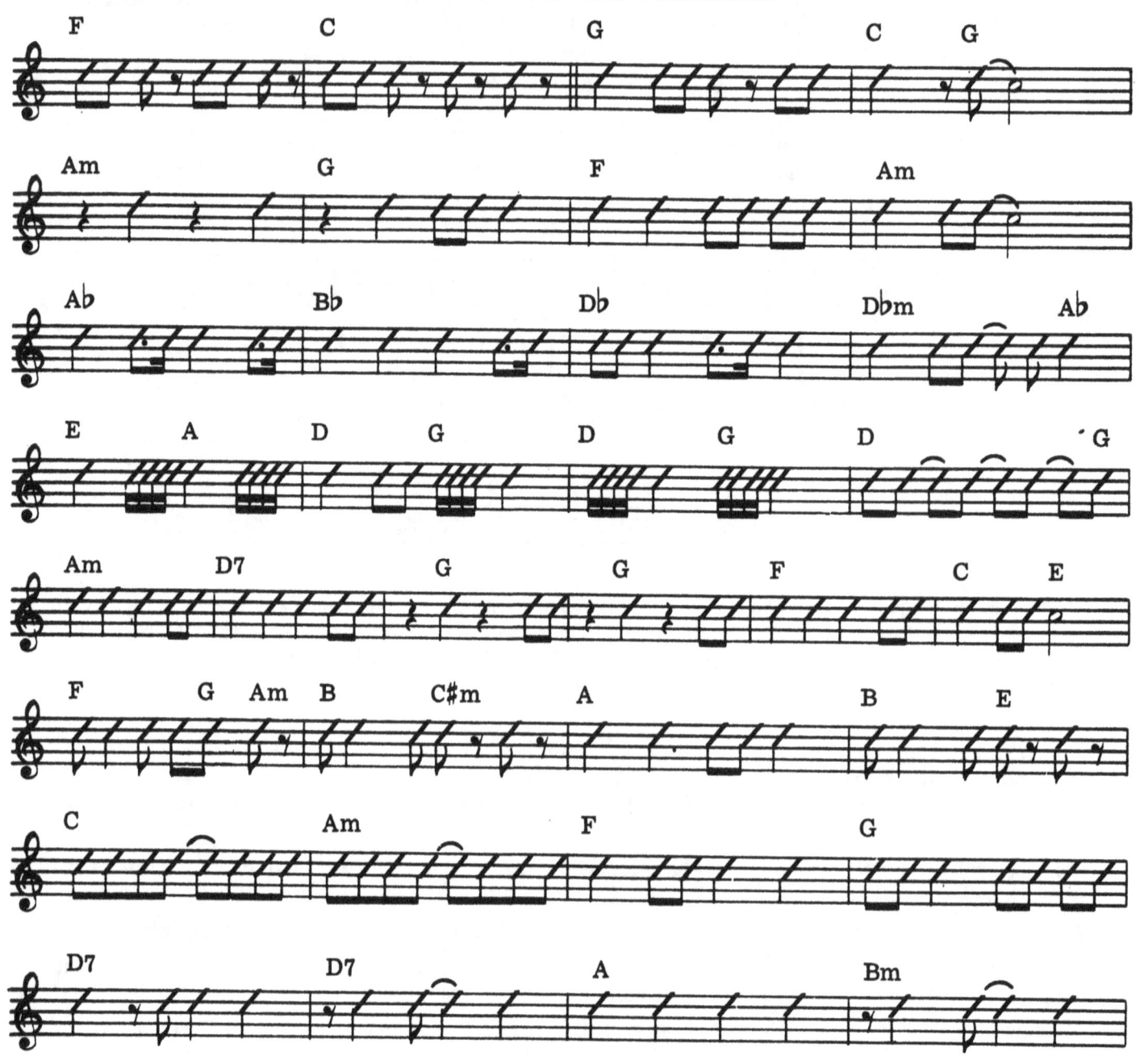

APPENDIX

The purpose of this appendix is to explain how and why our western European music system (which is what you have been playing and studying here, as opposed to Indian or Oriental musics) came into being, and how it works.

Our first section will deal with acoustics (the study of sound) and how it contributed to our system of notes. Then we will discuss Man and his history in discovering and organizing these tones. Our final section of this appendix will cover the theory and workings of our musical system today.

All of the topics here will be dealt with in a simple straight-forward manner. The design of this appendix is to simplify a mass of interrelated, but confusing, information into some useful Knowledge. The long winded ambiguous verbosity (B.S.) has been kept to a minimum. Read through the whole appendix. If you are unsure of some fact, reread the appendix again. Take your time and understand the application of each idea. It is the foundation of everything you will ever do in your music. Good Luck!

ACOUSTICS – THE SCIENCE OF SOUND

If you recall, in the beginning of the book we divided all sound into two categories, noise (irregular vibration) and tones (regular vibration). Acoustics can deal with both of these areas. However, here we will be talking about tones only.

Scientific experiment has confirmed the following facts:

Each note (or pitch) has a specific mathematical frequency at which it vibrates. If you say A has a frequency of 440 cycles per second (c.p.s.), you mean it vibrates back and forth 440 times in each second; and gives off some tone which we hear, in the process.

The speed at which a vibrating medium (like a guitar string) vibrates at, is related to the length of the string and the tension it is stretched to. The tighter you turn your guitar strings when you put them on, the higher the pitch. The shorter you make the string, by pushing down on a fret, the higher the pitch. You can see that no matter how hard you hit the string, you cannot really change the pitch. (You can create a slight "out of tuneness" however.)

While each tone sounds as if it is only one pitch, it is really a collection of many little pitches called "PARTIALS", (meaning part of), or "HARMONICS" (strictly speaking a harmonic is some note that vibrates at a precise multiple speed of the original tone – 4 is a multiple of 2).

FUNDAMENTAL:

In music theory, it is the original pure tone in a series of tones. It will have the lowest vibrating speed of all the tones.

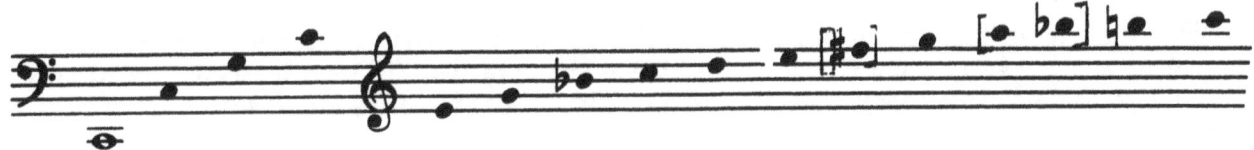

Fundamental   Partials – – – – – – – – – – – – – – – – – –

The bracketed tones are not really found in our system of tones today. These bracketed notes are a little 'flat' – more will be said on this under the section "Temperance."

Not all of these partials get equal volume in our tone. Some instruments favor some partials over others. This is part of the reason why a tuba does not sound like a guitar. (The other part of the reason is that individual instruments contribute certain kinds of noise in varying quantities. It is this noise that gives 'presence' to musical sounds, it is the "reedy" sound of the clarinet, and so on.)

In musical tones we observe that certain note partials occur more frequently than others. The "C" partial occurs the most. Then the "G" is the most dominant. With the exception of octaves, the most forceful dominating movement from note to note is the distance from G down to C. This is because we hear the "G" partial so strongly in our "C" note.

And now to some history . . . . .

Pythagorus was a Greek mathematician who lived from about 582 to 507 B.C. He performed many experiments and discovered several mathematical principles which are still valid today. Among his many experiments were some efforts with musical tones. He took two strings of animal gut of equal thickness and stretched them between two posts so that they were of equal length, and producing the same sound (pitch). By the use of a movable bridge he proceeded to alter the length of one of the strings. He found the following results: When string #2 was exactly half the length of #1, it gave off a very strong similar tone. When #2 was 2/3 the length of #1, it gave off a second different, but strong tone. He had discovered the octave and the 'fifth.' By starting with his second note (the 2/3 length which sounded the fifth) and dividing it in 2/3, he was able to find a second 'fifth.' (These 'fifths' will be explained in a minute.)

The first new note at 1/2 the distance became known as the octave. The second new note discovered (at 2/3), turned out to be the fifth note of our eight note scale.

```
              1   2   3   4   5        G is the fifth of the C SCALE or
C   D   E   F   G   A   B   C   D   E   F   G    G is a "fifth note" up from C and
1   2   3   4   5                      a "fifth" below D.
```

If we call the note he began with C in our scale system of today, then these are the notes he discovered:

```
                                          F#
                                      B
                                  E
                              A
                          D
                      G
                  C
```

He then applied his half string length idea to get the notes closer to each other (he brought them down an octave) and arranged them in ascending order and discovered:

G A B C D E F# G   !!!!!!!!!!

(known today as the G major scale)

What the Greeks had was our basic eight note diatonic scale. They measured the difference between G and A, and between B and C, and found that there were two different intervals. Eventually all of the twelve tones we use today were 'discovered' and arranged and organized into a tonal system like we have today.

By starting to play this scale on different notes in the scale, the Greeks were able to develop six other scales, known as 'Modes.' They are shown below.

C D E F G A B C	The Ionian mode (our major scale)
D E F G A B C D	The Dorian mode
E F G A B C D E	The Phrygian mode
F G A B C D E F	The Lydian mode
G A B C D E F G	The Myxolydian mode
A B C D E F G A	The Aeolian mode
B C D E F G A B	The Locrian mode

These modes are used today, in some of our music. As you get more advanced you will begin to use them if you don't already.

Today we have determined that the octave is a ratio of 2:1 to the original note. That is, the octave will vibrate at double the speed of the original note if it is above it, and it will vibrate at one-half the speed of the original note if it is below it.

If you have an A note at 440 c.p.s., then other A notes can be found at 220, 110, and 55; also at 880 and 1760.

Temperance, please . . .

Below is the mathematics of the 2/3 system:

GIVEN — the people of the world like A at 440 c.p.s. So we find an A at 110. 440 − 2 = 220; 220 − 2 = 110 c.p.s.   110 − 2/3 (the string) = 110 x 3/2 = 110 x 1.5 = 165.   So . . .

A = 110

110	x 1.5 = 165 (E) (the fifth above A)	
165	x 1.5 = 247 (B) (the fifth above E)	
247	x 1.5 = 370.5 (F#)− 2	= 185.35 (F#)
370.7	x 1.5 = 555.75 (C#) − 2	= 277.8 (C#)
277.8	x 1.5 = 416.7 − 2	= 208.35 (G#)
208.35	x 1.5 = 312.6	= 312.6 (D#)
312.6	x 1.5 = 468.9 − 2	= 234.45 (A#)
234.45	x 1.5 = 351.7 − 2	= 175.83 (E* or F)
175.83	x 1.5 = 263.75	= 263.75 (C)
263.75	x 1.5 = 395.63 − 2	= 197.81 (G)
197.81	x 1.5 = 296.72	= 296.72 (D)
296.72	x 1.5 = 445 − 2	= 222.53 (A)
222.53	x 1.5 = 333.795	= 333.795 (E)

if A = 110   then 110 x 2 = A octave = 220
            but 220   ≠   222.53

E = 165   but 2 x 165 = 330
          330   ≠   333.795:

We have reduced all these different notes by some multiple of two to get them into the same octave. Lo and behold, the octaves are not exact multiples of each other!!!

As it turns out, the 2/3 division isn't exact to the decimal points, so computing the octave this way results in "out of tune-ness" to our modern ear. The nations of the world had argued and 'mathematized' themselves into a "tempered system." By shaving a little off each fifth, the octaves come out in tune. (Bach's Well Tempered Clavier was a piano piece written to demonstrate the good aspects of this tuning system.)

So what does this prove? Well, for instance, when you tune your guitar, would it be easier to hear "tempered" fifths, or even octaves?

OUR SYSTEM OF HARMONY AND THEORY TODAY

Once our culture got the 12 different tones . . .

C C# D D# E F F# G G# A A# B

they organized them into a system of scales based on this order of tones . . .

C D E F G A B C

(and the six other modes which we have already seen).

But with our knowledge of acoustics, what else can we do in organizing these pitches?

INTERVALS . . .

As we have said, the word interval is used to describe distances between notes. When you measure distances in your back yard, you use units of length called "feet," "inches," or "yards." In music we have different units of length, which were originated long ago from our Diatonic scale.

C	D	E	F	G	A	B	C
1	2	3	4	5	6	7	Octave

The notes IN THE SCALE have been assigned numbers. The distance from C to E is called a "third" (count the notes including the one you started on); C to F is a "Fourth," and so on. To determine the distance between any two notes, imagine that the first note (usually the lower note, or note earlier in the alphabet) is the first note of its own diatonic scale. Then count up to the second note — and that's the interval.

```
      C#     D#          F#     G#     A#          Not a Diatonic Scale —
  C  |   D  |   E   F  |   G  |   A  |   B   C     but showing all the
      Db     Eb          Gb     Ab     Bb          half steps
```

If we count C to E, and A to C, we see that they are both thirds. However, looking at the half steps between the notes, we see that C to E has 5, while A to C has only 4!! While they are both thirds, they are not the SAME 'Third.' This occurs on other intervals in the scales too, so another part was added to the name of the distances between notes. We know there is a numerical part (second, third, or fourth, etc.) but there is also a "quality" (big or little) part of the name. For instance,

"C to E is a MAJOR Third."   "A to C is a MINOR Third."

How does this work??

Everything comes from that old Major diatonic scale. So let's get familiar with it.

These are the names of the intervals.

C to D	Major Second	C to A is a Major sixth
C to E	Major Third	C to B is a Major seventh
C to F	Perfect Fourth	C up to C is a Perfect Octave
C to G	Perfect Fifth	The word perfect is a holdover from Medieval days. It is actually the same as Major; but use it ONLY to describe 4ths and 5ths.

THE INTERVAL NAMES

```
 1   Db   2   Eb   3        4   Gb   5   Ab   6   Bb   7        8
 C        C#   D   D#   E    F   F#   G   G#   A   A#   B        C
```

DIATONIC (IN THE MAJOR SCALE) INTERVALS		NON DIATONIC INTERVALS		NON DIATONIC INTERVAL EQUIVALENTS
C–C Prime-Unison	(The Same Note)			
C–D Major 2nd		C Db Minor 2nd	OR	[C C#] Aug. Prime
C–E Major 3rd		C Eb Minor 3rd	=	C D# Aug. 2nd
C–F *Perfect 4th		[C Fb] Dimin. 4th	OR	[C E#] Aug. 3rd
C–G *Perfect 5th		C Gb Dimin. 5th	=	C F# Aug. 4th
C–A Major 6th		C Ab Minor 6th	=	C G# Aug. 5th
C B Major 7th		C Bb Minor 7th	=	C A# Aug. 6th
C C Octave		[C Cb] Dimin. Octave		[C B#] Aug. 7th

Now some rules to find our other intervals:

1. If any MAJOR interval is made SMALLER by one half step, the new resulting interval shall be called MINOR. C to E is Major third. C to Eb is Minor third.

2. If any PERFECT interval is made SMALLER by one half step, the new resulting interval shall be known as "DIMINISHED." C to G is a Perfect fifth. C to Gb is a Diminished fifth.

3. *If any MINOR interval is made one half step smaller, the new resulting interval is also known as "DIMINISHED." A to C is a Minor third. A to Cb is a Diminished third.*

   *Don't worry about this now — there will be more later . . .

4. If a MAJOR, OR PERFECT interval, is made one half step LARGER, the new resulting interval is called "AUGMENTED." C to A is a Major sixth. C to G is a perfect fifth. C to A# is an augmented sixth. C to G# is an augmented fifth.

**Octaves and unisons (unison is the same pitch, that is, a guitar and piano both playing middle C at the same time, would be said to be "playing in Unison") are known as "Perfect Intervals."

5. C to F# is an Augmented fourth. C to Gb is a Diminished fifth. These two intervals sound the same. Why the two different names? (This is an old hang-up but still in existence.) The # implies that you RAISED the F to F# (Augmented) while the b implies that you LOWERED the G to Gb (Diminished). It is still considered bad manners, and incorrect, to call C to F# a diminished fifth.

6. C up to E is a major third. E down to C is a major third. E up to C is a minor sixth. C down to E is a minor sixth.

   Beware of confusion!!! Try always to measure 'up' . . . be consistent!

MAJOR AND MINOR TONALITY . . . .

TONALITY: All harmony relating back to the tonic note, or chord of a key. (We will take 'harmony' to mean the combination of notes or chords — that's all. It could be diatonic, or non-diatonic.)

C	D	E	F	G	A	B	C
		A	B	C	D	E	F	G	A
		A	B	C#	D	E	F#	G#	A

The first scale above is a C major scale. The second is the Greek mode of the C scale beginning on A. (It has a very different sound.) The third scale is an A major scale.

Through hundreds of years of practice, the second scale has come to be considered so unique that it is as important in its difference as the major scale. It is known today as the 'natural' minor scale. If we compare the A natural minor scale, and the A major scale, we see that the third and sixth degrees of the major have been lowered a half step each (made MINOR intervals)*. That difference is the characteristic difference in sound that distinguishes Major Key sounds from Minor Key sounds. This minor scale can have chords built on it, harmony, and all the other properties that we have the Major scale. The only difference is the sound.

And that is what we mean by 'tonality.' It is the total sound of a progression of notes or chords. So if we move notes and chords built on the minor scale, we have a 'Minor Tonality.' If we move in the major scale, we have a 'Major Tonality.'

*The fact that the seventh is also lowered is of course important, but does not enter into our discussion of major and minor at this point.

In our western European music there are two kinds of 'tonality,' Major, and Minor. The categorization of the music depends on what scale it is based. If it is based on a major scale, then it is Major. If it is based on a minor scale with that different, darker sound, then it is considered minor. This darker sound is a result of a *b*3 and *b*6 in the scale. The difference is in the sound. In playing it on the guitar, if you play the C major scale starting on A, you are playing in a minor key . . . the Key of A minor.

If you can play a major scale, you can play a minor scale . . .

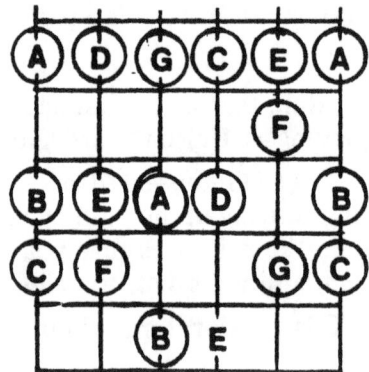

Let's combine the half step, whole step organization of our C scale, and the discovery of all these fifths by Pythagorus, and derive some new scales.

1	2	3	4	5	6	7	8				
C	D	E	F	G	A	B	C				
				G	A	ˌB	C	D	E	F	G

Given our first scale, we are going to build a new similar scale from the fifth degree.

This G scale is not the same as our C scale . . . All the intervals are the same except the seventh. It is a whole step here instead of a half step, as we decided it should be based on our Greeks, acoustics, and our ears. (Through history . . . Man has liked a half step from the seventh to the eighth note of the scale.)

We also know that we can have only one note in each scale with each letter of the alphabet (no G and G*b* in the same scale). So . . . we raise the seventh note of the scale up one half step, from F to F#.

This scale now fits all of our requirements for a scale like our C scale. It has the same half step whole step arrangement. It does not have two notes with the same letter in their names.

We can repeat this process, beginning on the fifth note of this G scale —

G   A   B   C   D   E   F#   G

D   E   F#   G   A   B ♮ C#   D

Once again the seventh degree of the scale had to be raised to fit our formula.

Below is the derivation of the rest of the scales with sharps.

C   D   E   F   G   A   B   C

G   A   B   C   D   E   F#   G

D   E   F#   G   A   B ♮ C#   D

A   B   C#   D   E   F#♮G#   A

```
A    B    C#   D    E    F#   G#   A
          E    F#   G#   A    B    C#♮D#   E
                    B    C#   D#   E    F#   G#♮A#   B
                              F#   G#   A#   B    C#   D#♮E#   F#
```

```
F#   G#   A#   B    C#   D#   E#   F#
          C#   D#   E#   F#   G#   A#♮B#   C#
```

Notice that in each instance the scale had to be altered to fit the whole step half step formula we have. And in each case it was the seventh step that had to be raised (♯ ed).

If we go any farther we'll be sharping notes already sharped . . .

What about that F note that was the second most dominant note in our original C scale?

```
     1    2    3    4
     C    D    E    F    G    A    B    C
                    F    G    A    B    C    D    E    F
```

Let's build some scales starting on the F note, and all other notes that appear as the FOURTH note of their scales.

Well, here the seventh degree is O.K. . . . But the fourth note is too high.

```
     F    G    A    B    C    D    E    F              F    G    A    Bb   C    D    E    F
```

In order to fit our formula of half steps and whole steps, the fourth must be lowered one half step:

```
               C    D    E    F    G    A    B    C
               F    G    A    Bb   C    D    E    F
```

Now it is correct. Let's repeat the process with this new scale.

```
          Bb   C    D♮Eb   F    G    A    Bb
```

Once again the fourth degree has to be lowered to fit our formula. Below are the rest of the scales that are derived from this effort, using the flat.

```
F    G    A    Bb   C    D    E    F
     Bb   C    D    E♮Eb   F    G    A    B
               Eb   F    G    A    Ab   Bb   C    D    Eb
                         Ab   Bb   C    D♮   Db   Eb   F    G    Ab
```

```
Db   Eb   F    Gb   Ab   Bb   C    Db
     Gb   Ab   Bb   C♮   Cb   Db   Eb   F    Gb
               Cb   Db   Eb   F♮   Fb   Gb   Ab   Bb   Cb
```

We must stop here because we will begin flatting notes already flatted.

In this situation the fourth degree of each scale had to be lowered in order to create a scale that met with the half step, whole step formula.

If you examine all of these scales, you'll see we have one beginning on each of our notes.

THE SCALES, THEIR SHARPS
FLATS, AND KEY SIGNATURES

C D E F G A B C   Key of C

G A B C D E F# G   Key of G

D E F# G A B C# D   Key of D

A B C# D E F# G# A   Key of A

E F# G# A B C# D# E   Key of E

B C# D# E F# G# A# B   Key of B

F# G# A# B C# D# E# F#   Key of F#

C# D# E# F# G# A# B# C#   Key of C#

F	G	A	B♭	C	D	E	F	Key of F

B♭	C	D	E♭	F	G	A	B♭	Key of B♭

E♭	F	G	A♭	B♭	C	D	E♭	Key of E♭

A♭	B♭	C	D♭	E♭	F	G	A♭	Key of A♭

D♭	E♭	F	G♭	A♭	B♭	C	D♭	Key of D♭

G♭	A♭	B♭	C♭	D♭	E♭	F	G♭	Key of G♭

C♭	D♭	E♭	F♭	G♭	A♭	B♭	C♭	Key of C♭

NOTATION FOUND
THROUGHOUT THE MUSIC COMPOSITION

(A)   Rehearsal letters are used to mark off large sections of music and make them easy to find.

Measure numbers are also used to keep track of where you are.

REPEAT MARKS

1. Da Capo — abbrev. D. C.

Go back to beginning of section and play through as before.

2.

Two signs used together; play along till ⊕ then go back to 𝄋 and repeat from there. Then continue on.

3. Dal Segno — abbrev. D. S. — used occasionally instead of ⊕ above.

4.

This sign is used to indicate that you repeat whatever is between the two. This sign is not a BAR LINE, and can appear in the MIDDLE OF A BAR, as well as coinciding with bar lines.

OR

OR

90

5.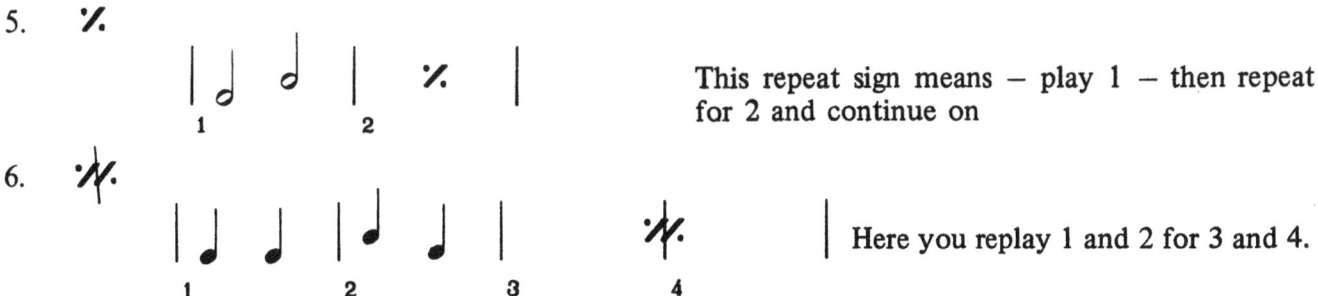

This repeat sign means – play 1 – then repeat 1 for 2 and continue on

6.

Here you replay 1 and 2 for 3 and 4.

This sign may also be used to repeat more than two bars as shown below.

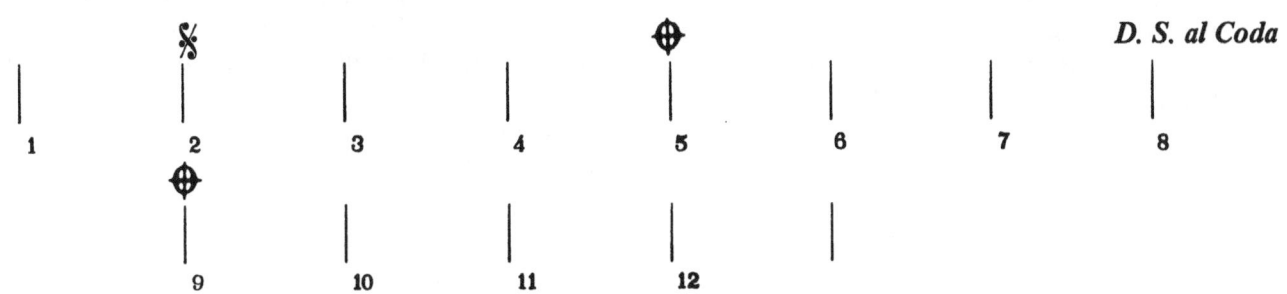

Here you would p ay 1 through 5 then repeat those for 6 – 10.

7. D. S. al Coda

D. S. al Coda

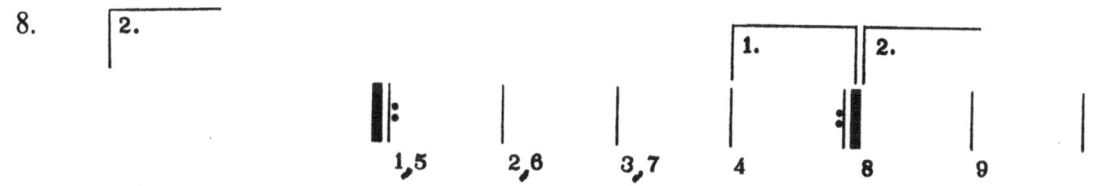

Play 1 – 8, then go back to 2 and play again till 5; then jump down and play section marked ⊕

8.

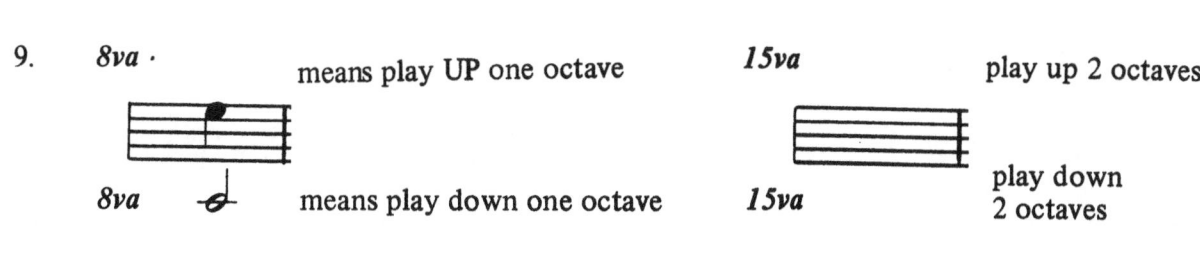

Play measures 1, 2, 3, and the "first ending" (4) then repeat 1 – 3 and take second ending. (You'll be playing measures 5, 6, 7, then 8 and 9.)

9. *8va ·*   means play UP one octave   *15va*   play up 2 octaves

8va   means play down one octave   *15va*   play down
2 octaves

EPILOGUE

Reading music can be very hard to learn, if you don't use common sense. It has been my goal in this book to show you how to use your head to educate yourself in reading music. I have tried to provide many different ways to understand and organize reading, and the various techniques it requires, so that you can confidently deal with any new situation you may encounter.

Try to read as much outside material as possible. Write down any troublesome situation you find. This will help you eliminate that 'fear' a person often feels when sight reading. There are many trumpet, flute, saxaphone, clarinet, and violin books you may use to practice your reading at this time. We are currently writing additional guitar manuscripts that will be tailored to the special problems of the guitar.

I hope this book has helped you understand reading music, and dispelled some of the mystery and fear that has surrounded reading on the guitar for so long. Thank you for the time and effort you have given my book. Please write me in care of the publisher with any questions or comments you may have, on any aspect of this book.

Sincerely,
Leon R. White